SAHARA MAN

By the same author
The Tuareg: People of Ahaggar

SAHARA MAN

Travelling with the Tuareg

Jeremy Keenan

JOHN MURRAY
Albemarle Street, London

First published in 2001
by John Murray (Publishers) Ltd,
50 Albemarle Street, London W1S 4BD

A catalogue record for this book is available from the British Library

ISBN 0-7195-6161 2

Typeset in Monotype Bembo 12/13.5
by Servis Filmsetting Ltd, Manchester

Printed and bound in Great Britain by
St Edmundsbury Press Ltd,
Bury St Edmunds, Suffolk

To Zandra, my wife, and our two children,
Mark and Charlotte, who never cease to amaze

Contents

Contents

Illustrations

(between pages 114 and 115)

All the photographs were taken by the author

Acknowledgements

Although this book is a travel story and not an academic study, I am grateful to several friends and colleagues in academia, namely Hugh Roberts, Christopher Chippindale, Stephen Hugh Jones, David Seddon, Helen Watson and George Joffe, for their help, friendship and advice.

An especially big 'thank you' is due to Jonathan Pegg, my literary agent at Curtis Brown, for his much-valued support (and very good lunches), and to Caroline Knox, commissioning editor at John Murray, for 'taking a risk'.

This also gives me the opportunity to thank other people whose help, at one time or another, is reflected in the outcome of this journey, namely Ian Lantham (GP), Schalk Visser, Tom Metcalf, and the late Johannes Nicolaisen and his wife Ida.

I would like to acknowledge the support of the British Academy and the Leverhulme Trust. I would also like to thank Helen Long at the Royal Botanic Gardens, Kew, who helped me unravel the mysteries of *efelehleh*.

Above all, I owe a great debt to the Tuareg. Memories of former generations inspired this journey, while the friendship extended to me by those mentioned in the text, especially Mokhtar and Claudia Bahedi, made it possible.

A more accomplished wordsmith could express more appropriately my feelings towards Algeria and its many brave and long-suffering people. I first set foot in the country shortly after it had experienced one of the most vicious wars in modern history, in which more than a million people were killed. But I found neither recrimination nor bitterness, only the hospitality and friendliness of people who, as one young man said to me, do not forget but are able to forgive. Returning to Algeria more than thirty-five years further on in its tortuous history, I was touched anew by the courtesy, charm and indeed affection of its people, even though they are once again experiencing troubled and difficult times. I make no attempt to explain those troubles – that is something even experts find difficult! I merely hope that my story may in some small measure help ensure that the people of Algeria are judged fairly rather than harshly by the outside world: now, as in the past, they have so much to offer.

Finally, I must thank Liz Robinson for helping to put the shine back on some rusty nuts and bolts. She made the hard work of editing fun and contributed to what today's fashionable parlance calls my 'life-long learning'.

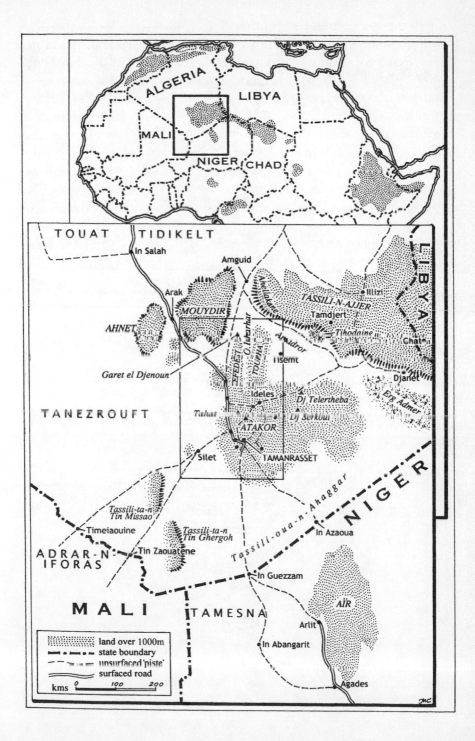

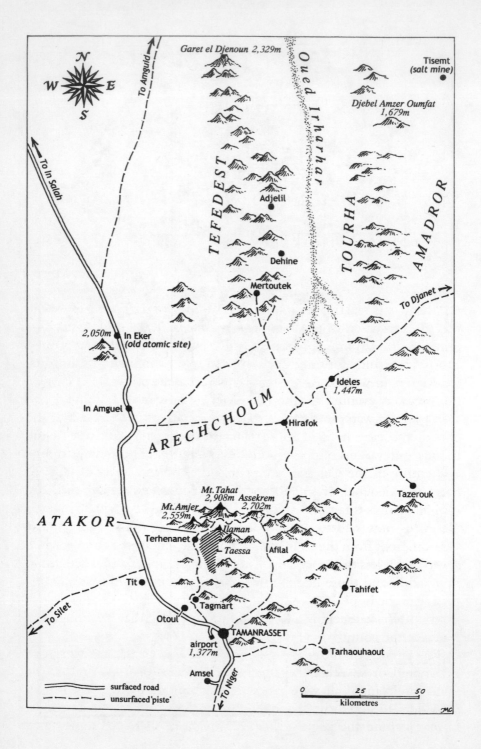

N
W E
S

To Amguid

Garet el Djenoun 2,329m

Oued Irharhar

Tisemt
(salt mine)

Djebel Amzer Oumfat
1,679m

T E F E D E S T

Adjelil

T O U R H A

A M A D R O R

Dehine

Mertoutek

To In Salah

To Djanet

2,050m In Eker
(old atomic site)

Ideles
1,447m

In Amguel

A R E C H C H O U M

Hirafok

Mt. Tahat
2,908m Assekrem
2,702m

Tazerouk

A T A K O R

Mt. Amjer
2,559m

Ilaman

Terhenanet

Taessa

Afilal

Tit

Tahifet

To Silet

Tagmart

Otoul

TAMANRASSET

airport
1,377m

Tarhaouhaout

Amsel

To Niger

surfaced road

unsurfaced 'piste'

0   25   50

kilometres

Prologue

Ahaggar
a desert island

THERE WAS STILL at least another half-hour of darkness before the gloomy dawn would begin to compete with the floodlights illuminating the airport's apron area. And it was wet: it had been raining almost incessantly for three days, so I was told, which was not unusual for Algiers in winter. As we approached the airport at Dar El Beida the previous evening on the Air Algérie flight from London I had seen pools of water scattered across the plain that stretches out to the east of the city. It filled the drainage ditches and gathered in the muddy excavations of the hundreds of building sites standing forlorn and empty in the wet as if aware that they would never be able to meet the demand of the thousands of people swarming into the capital. Algiers is fast becoming one of the world's big cities: its population is now said to number around five million, possibly more, very different from the time of Algerian independence in 1962, when it was much less than a million. On top of the rapid natural growth in population and those drifting into the city from the hills and countryside in the hope of economic betterment, the city is now facing an influx of *déplacés* seeking a haven from the killing that has ravaged so much of the country over the last few years.

The rain fell on me as I stood on the puddled tarmac, waiting with a hundred or so other passengers for permission from one of the many policemen, all with rifles or machine-guns slung over their shoulders, to step forward and identify our baggage, strewn across the tarmac behind the plane. It had clearly been there for some time, soaking up both the water from the puddles in which it was standing and the rain that showed no signs of abating.

My first reaction on seeing the luggage on the tarmac was to curse the fact that I was travelling in a Moslem country during the Holy month of Ramadan. You can identify which month is Ramadan merely by looking at national economic output figures: they take a dip. I assumed the baggage-handlers had simply downed tools for *sehor*, the meal taken just before sunrise that was to see them through *karem*, the day-long fast which is not broken until after sunset. Then the penny dropped, and I realised that baggage identification on the runway was all part of the almost paranoid security measures now enveloping Algeria which bring home to visitors that the country is in a state of what the foreign press, for want of more informative analysis, refer to as 'civil war'. Since the Algerian military annulled the results of the general election held at the beginning of 1992, which would have brought to power the world's first democratically elected Islamist government, Algeria has been in a state of crisis, one in which at least 100,000 people have been killed. Of these, I am told, some thirty per cent have been the victims of what the French-language press calls *l'arme blanche* – cold steel, a collective term for knives, axes, machetes and the like. Being shot is one thing; having one's throat slit strikes me as an altogether more gruesome way to die – the French word *égorger* seems to capture the reality a little better.

After identifying my baggage I carried it to the pile destined for Tamanrasset and, oblivious to my wet state, boarded the plane, a 737 that had seen better days. Though seats were not formally allocated, I had a strong sense of being ushered by the steward into the seat next to the emergency exit. Glancing around, I could see that I was the only foreigner on board; not surprising, as Algeria is still a 'no-go' area for tourism, subject to strict visa requirements. Was my seating just chance, I wondered? Or was it perhaps a gesture of gratitude towards a foreigner who was daring to travel in a country desperately trying to present itself to the outside world as normal; not that nine personal baggage or body searches between entering the airport building and boarding the plane could be called *normal*.

By the time the plane took off, two hours behind schedule, the grey light of the cold, wet dawn had broken. It made little difference: the drizzle and low cloud obscured almost all visibility. Within seconds we were in the cloud and banking to the north, out across the Mediterranean, thereby avoiding *Le Triangle de la Mort* – the Triangle of Death, the sinister name given to the central Mitidja region, sometimes known as the Blida Plain, between Algiers and the foothills of the Atlas, where many of the more gruesome massacres characteristic of Algeria's 'civil war' have taken place.

A strange thing about the take-off from Algiers airport was that within a few minutes the fear which had been gnawing away inside me for some little time had disappeared. For weeks I had been half hoping that the whole mad idea of returning to the central Sahara would have to be cancelled: either my visa application would be rejected, or my insurance company would get wise to the fact that Algeria was now on the Foreign Office list of 'stay away' countries. Neither had transpired, and now that I was airborne, there was nothing more I could do about it. I no longer had any control over my immediate destiny: I was bound for the great Central Sahara massif of Ahaggar, an area the size of France topped by volcanic peaks rising to almost ten thousand feet, and its administrative capital Tamanrasset.

The mountains of Ahaggar and the surrounding plateaux and escarpments of the Tassili are the traditional home of the Kel Ahaggar and Kel Ajjer Tuareg (*Kel* = people of), the blue-veiled, nomadic warlords of the Central Sahara.

I first travelled among them in 1964, thirty-five years ago, as an eager young geographer-cum-anthropologist. Initially I was attracted to the blue-veiled men of the Sahara, as the Tuareg were depicted, by their legendary status: they were the people of *Beau Geste*, greatly romanticised, especially by the French, whose colonial expansion into the Sahara in the nineteenth century was held in check for more than twenty years by their military prowess. Above all, and behind all the myths, legends and perceptions, was the fact that the Tuareg were different: they stood out from all the other peoples of the Sahara. First of all, the Tuareg are Berbers, not Arabs. Descended from the indigenous pre-Arabic peoples of North Africa, they speak a Berber language, Tamahak, which bears no relationship to Arabic. Unlike those of the many Arab tribes of the Sahara and other Islamic countries, Tuareg women, renowned for their beauty, are not veiled; rather, it is the men who veil their faces, traditionally in the

3

indigo-dyed cotton cloth that turns their skin an inky colour. Tuareg society was radically different from that of other peoples of the Sahara in that it was organised on predominantly matrilineal lines – 'It is the stomach', as all Kel Ahaggar say, 'that colours the child.' And, to cap it all, the Tuareg considered themselves not only invincible but, like the Masai of East Africa and the Zulu of South Africa, inherently superior to other men: they were the warlords of the Central Sahara and the guardians of its main trade routes. No one, not even the French, who established themselves in Algiers in 1830, entered the great desert citadel of Ahaggar without their permission. The first French military column that dared to do so, in 1881, was butchered with a ruthlessness that sent shock waves throughout France. The incident is still spoken of and laughed about by Tuareg today.

When I first visited the Tuareg of Ahaggar in 1964, I had already heard rumours that they were in revolt against the newly independent Algerian government. Over the next seven years I returned repeatedly, living in their semi-nomadic camps, learning about their culture and way of life and becoming their friend. This great warrior aristocracy, finally defeated by France in 1902 and subjected to sixty years of colonial rule, was by that time on its knees, struggling for survival after several years of drought had exacerbated the exigencies of a new political order whose decrees had stripped it of most of its traditional rights. Yet such adversity had scarcely dimmed the arrogance and aloofness of this haughty people. Noble Tuareg, their veils worn high, their demeanour and deportment reflecting their proud ancestry, stood out commandingly as they strolled through the streets of Tamanrasset, notwithstanding their anachronistic appearance.

When I finally left Ahaggar in 1971, it was like saying goodbye to a second home, one in which I had done much growing up and had learnt a great deal. I thought then that I would probably never return and, as the years went by, my desire to do so diminished: it would be too sad to witness for myself the changes I had foreseen, to hear of the deaths of old people who had befriended me. Better to remain in the past and to live with my memories of the nomadic camps in which I had stayed and the nomadic families with whom I had lived. It became increasingly difficult to conceive of returning. Whenever it was suggested I had a ready excuse, until the onset of Algeria's 'civil war' in 1992 effectively closed the region entirely and obviated the need for one.

Now, perhaps ironically, that same 'civil war' was taking me back to Ahaggar, and the reason lay somewhere within the complex spectrum of human intellect, embracing both conscience and curiosity. Some months previously a friend had enquired whether the then-recent appointment of Abdelaziz Bouteflika as President of Algeria and the consequently anticipated winding-down of the 'civil war' might make it easier for people like me, who had once known the country, to return.

'Why do you ask?' I was immediately aware that his suggestion had found a chink in my mental self-defences.

'You were the first in when the French left in the sixties,' he replied. 'If you were able to go back now, you would be the first in again.'

His remark started me thinking, and asking questions about what had happened to the Tuareg in these intervening troubled years. The fact that I did not *know* made me feel slightly ashamed. It was, after all, thanks to them that I had been able to establish and benefit from a reputation as something of an 'expert' on the Sahara and its people. The least I could have done, it now seemed to me, would have been to keep myself appraised of their situation.

Nomads do not fit easily into the bureaucratic ways of modern governments. Almost without exception, and not surprisingly, the twentieth century was not kind to them. For the Kel Ahaggar, it was one in which their world was turned upside-down on more than one occasion. That any semblance of their traditional nomadic culture and way of life survived is testimony to their inherent resilience and fortitude. Forced by France to abandon their more rapacious habits and explore new means of supplementing their traditional semi-nomadic pastoralism, the Kel Ahaggar developed a caravan trade to the oases of Touat and Tidikelt to the north and to Niger in the south, trading locally-mined salt for millet. They also invited an ever-increasing number of black-skinned *harratin* cultivators to come into Ahaggar to develop and work the small areas of cultivable land on their behalf.

If the French had destroyed the Kel Ahaggar's notions of their own invincibility, Algerian independence in 1962 brought even greater shocks. As far as the Algerians were concerned, the Tuareg political and social system was outmoded. Government decrees led to an immediate social revolution: slaves were emancipated, land was reallocated, and privileged political rights were removed. On the economic front, drought took its toll, while a combination of mechanised transport, frontier controls and the deteriorating value of salt as against millet brought an end to the great caravans that had set off annually from Ahaggar to Niger.

I had lived with the Kel Ahaggar during these difficult years, observing the pressures and hardships inexorably pushing them, reluctantly, into an ever more sedentary way of life. It was a time of transition, full of moments of regret and of great sadness framed within a sense of inevitability. But for many of these tribesmen – such as Khabte ag Abahag, whose camp was so often my home – the difficult and painful transition from nomadism to the restrictions of village life was somewhat eased by the development of tourism. Hiring their camels to local tour operators and working as cameleers, guides, cooks and so forth provided a trickle of income sufficient to enable many to remain in their cherished mountain camps.

I had left Ahaggar in 1971 feeling that most of the five thousand or so Kel Ahaggar then living in the region had managed to adapt to the demands of Algeria's new social and political order, and that perhaps half of them, perhaps more, were managing to cling, albeit precariously, to their semi-nomadic way of life.

What I could not have foreseen, of course, was the crisis that overtook Algeria in the 1990s. As I tried to fathom the effect of the country's troubles in the north on the Algerian Sahara, it began to strike me that Ahaggar had once again become an island. Several hundred million years ago, as its ancient granite dome rose above the surrounding Silurian and Devonian seas, that was precisely what the region had been. For the ancestral Tuareg, too, Ahaggar was an island, an almost impenetrable fortress in the centre of this great desert. Now, Ahaggar was an island in an ocean of political instability and upheaval. Although largely confined to the north, Algeria's 'civil war' has resulted in the entire country being cut off from tourism and from most other international traffic. To the south and south-west, Tuareg uprisings in Niger and Mali in the late 1980s and 1990s effectively closed the frontiers for much of this time. To the east, Colonel Ghadafi's Libya has been constantly provoking unrest in her neighbouring territories and has been closed for much of this time, while

Chad has been in a state of almost permanent revolt. Completing the encirclement, further to the west, beyond the desolate wastes of Tanezrouft, the struggles of the Saharawi people and their Polisario Front have ranged over much of the Western Sahara. As a result, Ahaggar has in almost all respects been ring-fenced: it has become *terra incognita.*

The more I thought about the Sahara and about what might have happened to the Tuareg, the more I wanted to return. I needed to find out how the Tuareg I had known had been affected, both by the sudden curtailment of the tourism on which they had become so dependent, and by those waves of political instability washing over much of the Central Sahara. No one I spoke to seemed to know anything definite. All was rumour and hearsay: stories of warlords taking control of the Central Sahara; of Tuareg roaming the mountains of Ahaggar armed with Kalashnikovs, or *Kalachs* as they are known, and raiding trans-Saharan traffic in an apparent reversion to their traditional ways. Other sources said there were no more nomads in Ahaggar, as the Kel Ahaggar had been forced to abandon their tents and their semi-nomadic way of life – sometimes, so I was told, because soldiers had taken to visiting the camps when the menfolk were away and raping the women. It was all very disconcerting, and enough to convince me that I should travel once more through Ahaggar, if only to find out the truth behind these stories – and perhaps to lay a few ghosts of my own.

Now, as I peered out of the plane's window into the surrounding cloud on my way back to Tamanrasset, I was simply afraid that I would no longer be able to cope with the desert: its hardness, its cold, its extremes, and the long distances over harsh terrain I knew I would have to walk. I was afraid that my thirty-years-older body might just blow a fuse and pack up. I was afraid of the shock and the sadness of what I might find, and I was also afraid that I would not be able to understand whatever might greet me, afraid to find that all I had once known now belonged to another world. And I was afraid that, even if they were still alive, those Tuareg who had once befriended me would not remember me.

I

Arriving in a Saharan metropolis

WE HAD BEEN flying for almost an hour before the cloud broke and I could see the desert below. We were over Tademait, the vast and almost totally flat gravel-strewn plateau that separates the great sand seas of the northern Sahara from the low-lying depression of Tidikelt just to the north of Ahaggar. In pre-colonial times the well-watered oases of Tidikelt and the adjoining region of Touat, with their palm groves and gardens, were the main source of dates and cereals for the Tuareg of Ahaggar, who either traded with or raided their northern Arab neighbours, depending on their degree of hunger and hardship, and the prevailing state of relations between them.

My gaze wandered along dirt tracks that splayed out in their hundreds across the flat desert surface for dozens of miles in every direction, like a spider's web. Many a traveller has perished after being led astray among Tademait's countless will-o'-the-wisp trails. It looked as if many of the small hollows and depressions of the plateau's surface contained pools of water. Rain is rare in this part of the Sahara, but not unheard-of in winter. And if it had rained over Tademait, there was a good chance that rain had also fallen in Ahaggar, topping up the water-holes and thereby making travel there just a little bit easier.

As the plane banked to begin its descent for a scheduled stop at In Salah, the main oasis in Tidikelt, I finally spotted the new highway, where it sliced through the escarpment like a pencil-line and dropped down onto the sandy plain below. And just beside it I could make out where the *piste* – the old dirt track – had once snaked its way down from the plateau, to become buried under the shifting sands of Tidikelt. I thought of the many times I had travelled on that *piste*, and of the hours spent shovelling sand and laying metal sand-ladders too hot to touch in the searing heat, only to repeat the process all over again a few yards further on.

From the air, In Salah did not appear to have changed much. The pans of open water that stood incongruously on the desert's sandy surface seemed more extensive and the gardens that surrounded them more verdant than I had remembered them; probably looking down on them from the air caused them to stand out more sharply against the greys, yellows and browns of the desert. There was a handful of more modern-looking buildings in the town's small centre, and the road out to the airport was now tarmacked, but these few signs of modernisation were scarcely enough to suggest that In Salah would not one day be reclaimed by nature. Sand swept across the tarmac as it had across the *piste*, and sand dunes still piled up against the walls of the houses around the edge of the town, threatening to consume it altogether if the occupants ever relaxed their vigilance.

'You're with the oil companies?' the young Algerian sitting next to me asked in French.

'No,' I replied. 'Just a tourist.'

'You're going on to Tamanrasset, then,' he said in a matter-of-fact sort of way, as if no right-minded tourist would ever stop off at In Salah. In Algeria they say that no one ever goes to hell – they just get posted to In Salah. That probably sums it up. The temperature rises to around fifty degrees Celsius in summer, which seems to last for most of the year. Even breathing can become difficult: you have to consciously suck the burning hot, bone-dry air down into your lungs, which then feel as if they too are on fire. At night, you lie in the open for relief. I was once there when the Foreign Legion outpost was evacuated because of the extreme heat. But the heat is nothing compared to the sand, which is ever-present, ever-moving, attacking you and getting into absolutely everything, becoming part of your body and part of your diet. And as if that were not enough, there is the water: saline and sickly enough to make you vomit if you are not used to it. Even the melons and fruits grown in the gardens are imbued with salt.

'Why oil?' I asked. 'Have they found oil here?'

'Not oil, gas. Masses of it. In Salah is now the world's biggest gas producer.'

I had heard that British Petroleum had been given a contract four or five years ago to explore the area, but was doubtful about my travelling companion's claim. Maybe he was referring to what had been discovered, and meant it had the potential to become one of the world's largest gas fields. Anyway, whatever the facts, it seemed In Salah was now a place to be reckoned with.

Touching down on the baked airstrip, we taxied up to the tiny airport building. It looked much the same as I remembered it except for a handful of machine-gun-toting police, and these I was already beginning to accept as part of the new Algerian scene. A little way beyond the building a wind-sock, now hanging wanly on its pole, was a reminder of another of In Salah's manifold charms.

'I hope you enjoy your holiday in Tamanrasset,' the man next to me said as he got up to leave. He was not going to work in the gas fields, but returning home to spend the remainder of Ramadan with his family. He joined the awkward line of passengers pressing forward up the aisle with their miscellaneous assortment of hand luggage, and I watched as they ambled down the steps, unfazed by the armed security, then walked in single file across the short stretch of bright, sunlit forecourt to disappear through the door into the airport building. There would be new passengers, presumably mostly workers going home to Tamanrasset. As I savoured the few minutes of calm before they boarded, the smell of warm desert air slowly filled the cabin. In Arabic, *sahara* is the word for the colour of the desert. But to me *sahara* is also a smell, unlike that of any other desert I have known; now, for the first time in years, it was coming back to me. Indeed, it is almost a 'non-smell', difficult to describe, more a texture than an odour, like the rock dust from a limestone quarry: invasive, rasping, pungent, but devoid of scent.

As we sat there waiting I could feel the warm, dry dust penetrating ever deeper into the crevices of my lungs, defying them to waft it back out. Before we were airborne my chest had begun to seize up in protest. I couldn't blame it: from the snow of England through the rain and drizzle of Algiers to this, in a matter of twenty-four hours, was too much.

We took off from In Salah for Tamanrasset: fifty minutes' flying time, 658 kilometres by road, and uphill all the way.

The approach to Ahaggar is both magnificent and foreboding. First, the great wall of the Tassili escarpment looms – dark, intimidating, and seemingly impenetrable. Behind it are the mountain ranges that rise up like clusters of warts from the surface of the huge granite dome of Ahaggar: first the mountains of Mouydir, then the massif of Ahnet to the right and Tefedest to the left and, further on, the great volcanic peaks of Atakor, the highest mountains in Algeria.

As I looked down into the tangle of rocks and dry valleys I had once known so well, memories came flooding back, of the camps, the mountains, the water-holes, the lava-strewn wastes, the nooks and crannies where life was to be found. But it now looked horribly desolate and dry: I had never seen Ahaggar looking so parched. The rain that had fallen on Tademait had not after all reached this far south.

As the plane began its descent, I strained to catch a glimpse of Tamanrasset from the air. But just as its outskirts came into sight the plane banked sharply, leaving me with a window of empty pale blue sky. When we levelled up it was desert again, now rushing up to meet me. I had forgotten that the airport was some distance out of town.

As I stepped off the plane a policeman beckoned me. 'You are a tourist.' It was as much assertion as question, and before I had finished my confirmation I was being directed to follow him, to a spartan room off the arrival hall containing one table and two chairs. We sat facing one another, either side of the table, and he reached into a drawer. There was a strange black-and-white quality about the room, like something out of an old-fashioned cops and robbers movie, and I half-expected him to pull out a tape-recorder, place it on the table and begin an interrogation. 'What is your name?' he asked, and passed me one of the countless forms that make travel in Algeria a bureaucrat's dream. As I dutifully filled in the form he repeated my name, having the French-speaker's usual difficulty with 'Jeremy'. Did I detect familiarity or deference? Was it pleasure at the arrival of a rare tourist – or had he perhaps been briefed, and was expecting me? I had been advised in London that Algeria did not want people like myself, who knew the country, travelling around freely. If I was allowed in at all, my movements would surely be well monitored.

If the policeman had been expecting me, as I thought might be the case, he said nothing to give me cause for alarm. Like nearly all Algerians with whom I have been acquainted, he was the epitome of charming hospitality.

'Wait here for a moment,' he said, as he slipped my completed arrival form into the top drawer of the desk. 'I will get you a trolley.'

Within a minute he was back, having commandeered what I suspected was one of the airport's few serviceable luggage trolleys. Pushing it before me, I followed him through the crowded, dingy concourse. Eyes stared at me from beneath an array of head-dresses, making me even more conscious of being singled out.

Outside the airport building there was near gridlock: every waiting vehicle wanted to be within a yard or two of the exit doors. My personal policeman helped extricate a taxi from the ruck, and saw me off with a friendly wave. This was all very well, but I was left feeling disconcerted, wondering whether I was to be kept under surveillance, as those in London had suggested, or welcomed as the vanguard of the long-anticipated return of foreign tourists.

Soon we were onto a ten-kilometre stretch of surfaced dual carriageway. The old corrugated *piste* I had known so well (and which, according to a United Nations report I once read, had quadrupled the price of road transport to Tamanrasset) was nowhere to be seen. The new dual carriageway was the hot-rod stretch, the one place where enthusiasts could show off the paces of their vehicles. The new Toyota Land Cruisers which had clearly replaced camels, Land Rovers and all else as the ultimate form of desert transport were capable of European motorway speeds; for the old bangers held together with string and whatever else came to hand, it was sometimes not much more than walking pace. It was an open invitation, it seemed to me, to fatal pile-ups and death by misadventure for wandering pedestrians and goats. Speed, and perhaps even time, had now begun to mean something in this part of the Sahara.

I was relieved to reach the outskirts of Tamanrasset and the end of the dual carriageway, as my driver was obliged to slow to a more circumspect speed. I recognised nothing. The first wall we passed protected a cemetery, the next, on the other side of the road, a camping site-cum-leisure park. Then we came to a sizeable roundabout, another monument and a large sports hall, and signs in both French and Arabic directing traffic to 'Centre Ville', 'Toutes Directions', 'Zone Industrielle' and other places new to me. Beyond the roundabout, the road was bordered on either side by Dali-esque colonnaded pink-stuccoed pedestrian walkways drawing one in, like two great tentacles, towards a hidden centre. I had a sensation of not exactly *seeing* things, but of having a kaleidoscope of surreal images almost thrust before me. This was not the Tamanrasset I had known – this was a city, and one that was completely alien to me.

My first crossing of the Sahara to Tamanrasset in the summer of 1964 had taken nine days. When finally I reached the little town nestling in a small plain on the northern side of the *Oued* Tamanrasset, it seemed to me one of the most most beautiful places on earth. It was quiet, sleepy, and remote, all its buildings the same soft, terracotta-brownish-red colour. Not only was there no tarmac, there were no pavements. The main street and the few that ran off it were of compacted dirt under a veneer of dust and fine sand that swept imperceptibly from one side to the other, according to the wind. The tamarisk trees which shrouded the town, giving it an air and scent of freshness, also lined the streets. In most desert towns, trees are a rarity; here, their cool shade encouraged the townsfolk – no more than four thousand or so altogether – to spend more time in the conviviality of the public thoroughfares than behind closed doors.

No many Tuareg lived in Tamanrasset at that time, most preferring their semi-nomadic camps in the surrounding mountains. Those who did were mostly nobles who had latched on to the French colonial regime as interpreters, guides, overseers, and other quasi-administrative functionaries. They could often be seen sauntering elegantly in the main street, their heads totally veiled except for a narrow eye-slit. Beasts of burden – camels and donkeys, usually laden with precious firewood gathered from the surrounding mountains and valleys – and riding camels, sometimes splendidly adorned in traditional regalia, ranked equal with the town's few motor vehicles for right of way.

In those days a plane came from Algiers nominally twice a week (but more usually only once, depending on a whole host of ever more inventive excuses) delivering post and a very few passengers, and rarely keeping to anything like a schedule. The town had one small colonial-style hotel, a post office, what passed locally for a hospital, a dozen or more shops, one petrol station, and one café, the Café de la Paix.

*

Now, as we penetrated deeper into the urban unknown, traffic seemed to come at us from all sides: Land Cruisers by the dozen, yellow taxis everywhere (I later counted one hundred and ninety altogether), big trucks, smaller trucks, jalopies, pick-ups of every conceivable make and era, cars, mopeds and bicycles; but no camels. There were pedestrians by the hundred, uniformed traffic police – and goats, also by the hundred. Their job, I discovered, if they could stay alive, was to help out the town's refuse collectors. There was new building work going on as far as the eye could see: some finished, some half-finished, and some barely begun. Cement was clearly big business.

We turned on to an Inner Ring Road. Here at last there were tamarisk trees, and I began to get my bearings. We were crossing the *Oued* Sersouf, which on the rare occasions when it rained, drained water off the plain behind Tamanrasset. In the past it had marked the edge of town, the beginning of the desert; here nomads would 'park' their camels and offload their possessions before heading into town. Here I had taken my own camel and hobbled it, after buying it in the market just off the main street. Sersouf was no longer on the edge of town; on the contrary. Almost as far as the eye could see, both sides of the *oued* were now lined with buildings.

A new, long street, wider than the old main street, almost like a boulevard, stretched far away into the distance on the left. Decorative lights like those on a Christmas tree were swagged across the road. Funnily enough, they didn't seem out of place. The plethora of shops, offices and little businesses beneath them and a throng of people and traffic made it difficult to imagine that this had once been desert wasteland.

Traffic congestion prompted my driver to turn off the Inner Ring towards the old town centre. Suddenly, my surroundings became familiar. The old shops looked much as I had remembered them, though perhaps they were a little brighter, and had more goods on display. We turned on to the main street and I saw that the Café de la Paix was also still there, although at this time of day in Ramadan it was not doing any business. For the first time since stepping off the plane I felt the warm glow of recognition. What of Sliman, the café's proprietor, I wondered? He had looked after me all those years ago, and I remembered him as being an old man then. Was he still alive, or perhaps in retirement? The old Hôtel Amenukal, subsequently renamed Tin Hinane, had been my first port of call when I first arrived in Tamanrasset. The newly-independent Algerian government had been understandably reluctant to see the title of the Tuareg's supreme chief blazoned forth in the main thoroughfare, a symbolic reminder of traditional political rights and pre-eminence and possible focus for Tuareg discontent; the name of their legendary ancestress seemed a safe compromise. There it was, but it looked boarded-up. The old hospital next to it had been razed to the ground, probably no bad thing, and the empty ground was temporarily colonised by a number of goats. Signs advertising Air Algérie's offices stuck out from a couple of buildings. Also temporarily deserted because of Ramadan, a modern street café boasting outdoor television and psychedelic lighting occupied one corner of the main intersection, at the centre of which a traffic policeman whistled and waved his arms confusingly at almost everything that moved.

We drove on, past the old military fort, once the last outpost of a metropolitan power stretching from Dunkerque to Tamanrasset, past the Mairie and a few other buildings I recognised, towards the Hôtel Tahat. Built in 1978 when tourism in Ahaggar was reaching its peak, and named after the highest mountain in both Ahaggar and Algeria, Hôtel Tahat was about a kilometre beyond the town centre. Air Algérie's London office had confirmed that this was the only hotel in town, apart from the old Hôtel Tin Hinane, which no one apparently used any more. Later, exploring the suburbs, I came across two empty-looking buildings both displaying hopeful 'Hôtel' placards.

It was a little after midday when I checked in at the Hôtel Tahat. I saw no sign of human life apart from the two young women on the reception desk. They offered me a room with or without television, with or without a shower suite and toilet. The choice was a little overwhelming: I had never associated Tamanrasset with either. Then I realised that all the satellite dishes I had noticed on the drive across town must have been television receivers. I opted for the shower and declined the television: I had had enough shocks for one day. I filled in the standard forms and was taken to my room. The hotel was cold, and not one of its hundred or so rooms seemed to be occupied. This, I realised, was the devastating effect on tourism of Algeria's 'civil war'. The furniture in my room looked somewhat dilapidated and neglected, but it was clean and more than adequate for my needs. And the plumbing worked, to my surprise.

There was a tiny balcony overlooking the hotel's walled back garden. The bright sunlight was deceptive: even at this time of day it was not warm enough to make me discard my sweater. The 'garden' was more of a yard, mostly taken up with the hotel's septic tank system. The disconsolate body-language of two men working on it seemed to suggest that it was giving trouble. Beyond the garden wall a cluster of poplar trees marked the edge of the *Oued* Tamanrasset, its sandy bed at least a hundred metres wide. Here it was open season for the wind, and even as I watched an unending supply of rubbish, sand and dust was whipped up into a series of miniature whirlwinds that swirled like demons up and down the *oued*.

On the far side of the *oued*, where I remembered open desert, I could now see the traffic of the ring road and a large mechanical excavator working on a building site, seemingly hell-bent on competing with the *oued* as to which could create the most dust. Behind it, buildings stretched back to the top of a low ridge, which was the horizon.

Stepping back into my room, I lay down on the bed. I needed to gather my thoughts, and plan what I was going to do. I felt bewildered and disoriented by all I had seen since my arrival, and it was dispiriting not to know where or how to make a start. I could also feel signs of trouble in my chest. I had worked so hard to get fit; how ironic it would be if I had picked up an infection on the way here. My first task at least was clearly defined: I needed money, Algerian dinars. Given the country's closed economy and restricted currency exchange, these are not the simplest of things to acquire; I had already been obliged to leave an IOU at the hotel desk for the taxi driver who had brought me from the airport.

Forcing myself up from the bed, therefore, I donned a warm padded jacket and retraced my steps through the labyrinth of cold, empty corridors to the hotel lobby. Walking quickly, I could have made it from the hotel to the bank in ten minutes. But, like a sailor venturing ashore on sea-legs after a long voyage, I took my time. I needed to familiarise myself with my new environment: the texture of the pavements and the mud and stone walls, the fragrance of the tamarisks, the harsh dryness of the air, the snatched glimpses of people snatching a glimpse of me from behind doors half-ajar, and the stares of the children – who like children in almost every corner of the world showed no fear in their curiosity.

There had been no banks in Tamanrasset when I left in 1971; now there were four, including a branch of the Central Bank, the only one authorised to handle foreign exchange. There were no other customers, and as I settled down to the endless form-filling I was joined on the customers' side of the counter by the manager, a man of about my own age, dressed in sports jacket, slacks and open-necked shirt. As he stretched out a hand in greeting he used the other to remove a cigarette from his mouth, which was immediately transformed by an engaging smile. Before he had finished introducing himself he had picked up my passport and traveller's cheques, flipped through them and handed them to an assistant with an instruction to do all the paperwork.

'Come over here while you're waiting,' he said, offering me a cigarette, which I declined, and ushering me towards a corner where a cluster of leather chairs surrounded a glass-topped coffee table. I had a strong sense of a man used to greater responsibilities, bored by a job beneath his skills and experience, a man who craved contact with a more sophisticated world than was to be found in this remote desert town.

'This is your first visit?' he asked. His tone was in no way inquisitorial.

'No, but the first for almost thirty years.'

'That is amazing – you know Tamanrasset!'

'I did, but now I scarcely recognise it.'

'That is not surprising. Its growth in the last few years has been truly remarkable.'

'How big is it?' I asked.

He shrugged his shoulders and held out his hands: 'Eighty thousand, perhaps a hundred. It is more like a city; and forty-eight nationalities live here!' Sensing my incredulity, he began to reel them off: 'Niger, Mali, Libya, Burkina Faso, Nigeria, Senegal, Cameroon ...' He ran on through almost every country in Africa, and I realised he was also counting several ethnic groups, such as the Bambara, as countries. But he had made his point: Tamanrasset had become an international centre on the new map of Africa, especially important for all those peoples to the south who were trying to make it to the richer countries of North Africa, perhaps even on into Europe.

But I knew there was much more to the growth of Tamanrasset than pressure from Black Africa, particularly as most of the thousands of refugees who had poured into Tamanrasset in the 1980s and early

1990s following the uprisings of Tuareg against the governments of Mali and Niger had now been repatriated. I had a feeling there were many more complex reasons for Tamanrasset's extraordinary growth. I wanted to ask him how many people from the north had moved into the Sahara with their families, seeking safety from the troubles of the country's 'civil war'. I also wanted to know more about the enhanced importance of Tamanrasset as both the administrative and political centre of Algeria's extreme south and as a frontier garrison of some size and obvious military importance. But this was not the time to raise what I assumed were likely to be sensitive matters. Instead, I asked him about his home and family.

He told me about his daughter, the same age as mine and also in her first year at university, and his home town of Diskra, a town I had once visited, and remembered for its scenic location on the northern edge of the Sahara, at the foot of the Aures mountains.

We chatted for an hour or so, covering Algeria's War of Independence against France – mere history, now, for Algeria's rising generations; the first years of independence, when he was an economics student at Algiers university; my first journeys into the Sahara and to Tamanrasset. We both seemed more at home in the past than in the present. Only one person came into the bank during this time, and he waited no more than a few minutes before he was handed a huge pre-wrapped bundle of notes: tens, perhaps hundreds, of thousands of dinars. Seeing my curiosity, my newly acquired friend answered before I had time to ask how one could spend so much money in this town. 'He's from the Development Bank' – I had been there before coming in here – 'we supply them with their money.'

'And what do they do with it?'

'For all the various projects,' he replied nonchalantly.

When, finally, my money was ready, one of the bank clerks brought it to where we were sitting and handed it to the manager. As if introducing a prodigal son, he said to the clerk: 'You know, he was here thirty years ago.' Then, turning to me, he asked whether I knew Ideles, a small village 260 kilometres to the north-east of Tamanrasset. I had spent three days there in 1968. 'You know Barrère?' Yes, I told him, I had met Guy Barrère. He was a French schoolteacher who had married a Tuareg girl and ran a little village school in Ideles, with a small boarding-house for nomad children. 'Well,' said the manager, becoming even more excited and putting his hand on the clerk's shoulder, 'Mohammed here was at Barrère's school then.'

'Do you remember my visit, and the paintings?' I asked Mohammed.

'I was very small then. What were the paintings?'

'All the children made me pictures of themselves and their homes, with coloured crayons. It was a rather unprofessional test to see whether there was a difference in perceptions between nomad and village children.'

'And were they very different?' asked the manager.

'Extraordinarily so,' I said. 'The nomad children were preoccupied with the buttons on their new tunics – coming in from the desert, they'd never seen buttons before. They painted little black dots all over their clothes. And they were petrified of stairs – they thought wicked spirits lived beneath them. The town children's paintings were full of flowers.'

'Why flowers?' asked the manager.

'Poppies!' I replied. 'The most important thing for their fathers was the hash – marijuana – they grew it in their gardens.'

Mohammed laughed. 'I was one of the village children. It's still the same,' he said. 'Always the men growing their little bit of hash!'

It gave me a strange feeling to realise that bundled up in my attic at home was a painting that Mohammed had done for me as a six- or seven-year-old child.

I left the bank and walked the few hundred metres past the military barracks, the whistling traffic cop and the psychedelic café into the old main street. If I was to make head or tail of this extraordinary town, I need to start from a point of familiarity. At that moment, nothing was familiar except the original main street with its tamarisk trees, and perhaps, I thought, the old Café de la Paix, where I used to sit and eat almost every morning and evening when I was in town.

From the outside the café looked much the same, its entrance on the main street protected by two large tamarisks that kept it in perpetual shade. I put my head tentatively around the entrance. One side of the café was the original kitchen and eating area, which had held about four small tables – enough, in those days, for its meagre and infrequent clientele. Now, however, like the town itself, it had expanded, taking over the shop or room next door. Now there were at least a dozen tables, all empty at this time of day because of

Ramadan. The furniture and décor seemed much as I remembered, plastic and brightly-coloured, except for a photo-poster of Algeria's new president, Abdelaziz Bouteflika, on the wall. I don't recall ever seeing the smiling face of Ahmed Ben Bella, Algeria's first President, displayed in this way thirty years ago; but Tamanrasset wasn't politically switched-on in those days.

While I was looking around, wondering about Sliman, the owner, a young man who had followed me into the café asked if he could be of help. 'Is Sliman still the *patron*?' I asked. Would he know whom I was talking about?

'You want to see Suleyman? I will get him.' Before I had time to say anything more, he was gone, and a minute or two later Sliman – or Suleyman, as he now seemed to be called – appeared. I recognised him immediately. When I first knew him, I thought he was at least fifty: he was still thin and scrawny, but now looked no more than sixty. The growth and increased prosperity of Tamanrasset had obviously served him well.

I introduced myself, telling him I used to eat in his café almost every day back in the 1960s. I could see that he was struggling to remember me. Then he had a flash of inspiration: 'You wore a big beard?'

I had completely forgotten that beard. Of course he would not have recognised me. And to complete my disguise, I was now half-bald and a stone or two heavier. He seemed genuinely moved to see me, taking me by my arm and leading me into a back room. Soon we were talking about Tamanrasset as it used to be.

'Have you seen Beh yet?' he asked.

'Beh ag Ahmed? No, not yet. I've only been in town a couple of hours and I haven't seen anybody apart from the bank manager. I didn't know where to start looking, apart from coming here to find you.' Beh had been my *professeur*, as he liked to call himself. I had soon realised that if I wanted to study the Tuareg seriously I would have to learn their language, Tamahak, and would need to find someone who could teach me. Beh was then in his late thirties, recently widowed and keen, I suspected, to do something that would take his mind off his loss. Each morning I went to his house for about three hours for my 'classes'. Beh was a noble, a Kel Rela, and one of the few Tuareg who had settled in Tamanrasset. Even more exceptionally, he worked a small garden which he loved passionately. He said it gave him tranquillity. Traditionally, Tuareg despised manual labour, especially cultivation, which was undertaken on their behalf by slaves or *harratin*. But Beh's garden had been close to where, earlier, I had seen the excavator at work. I feared that it no longer existed, and wondered where he now lived.

'Come to dinner tomorrow evening,' said Sliman, as we stepped back onto the pavement. 'I see Beh most days in town and I'll tell him you are here. He will be pleased to see you.'

'Thank you,' I replied. I felt a little overawed that he should have invited me to his home in preference to the café, something he had never done in the past. 'But where do you live?'

'You don't know my house?' he asked, sounding a little surprised. 'It's just round the corner. Come, I'll show you now.' He took me down an alleyway that led off the main street a few yards beyond the café, left and then immediately right into a narrower alley bounded by old, terracotta-plastered walls through which doors opened onto little rabbit warrens of private courtyards and rooms. 'This is the door,' he said. 'Just come here tomorrow evening.'

As I made my *au revoir* and turned to leave, he said: 'My house is the oldest in Tamanrasset. Did you know that?'

I made my way back to the main street and meandered through a few of the shops. Thirty years ago they had stocked little beyond the basic necessities, and even those were often in short supply. But times had changed, and I could see that 'shopping' was rapidly becoming a leisure activity as much in Tamanrasset as in Toronto or Tunbridge Wells. The only thing I needed straight away was a hat. Later I would buy a few yards of cotton cloth to make a *chech*, as the Arabs called the Tuareg's head veil, to wear when I was travelling in the open desert, but for town use I wanted a hat. I would have liked a Panama, or even one of those Australian jobs, without the corks. A search of most of the shops in the centre of town failed to turn up either, however, and I had to make do with a hideous, 'made in Philippines' silver-grey baseball cap. Not even the most populist politician would have worn it.

I made my way slowly back to the hotel, wandering down backstreets and alleys, trying to get my bearings in all the new development and in the hope of finding places I remembered. I stopped only to buy a packet of biscuits and four oranges from a Libyan street vendor. He spoke only Arabic and, much to my amazement, good English.

The hotel was still cold and still empty. In my room, I wrapped myself in a blanket and lay on my bed as the last light of day faded. Seeing Sliman again and knowing that Beh was still alive and living in Tamanrasset had cheered me up, when everything else about being in Tamanrasset was depressing. I felt I had been subjected to a dramatically illustrated kill-or-cure crash course on raw, unregulated and unquestioned modernisation in which my attention had been drawn, almost subliminally, to all that most shocked me: satellite dishes perched incongruously on top of mud-brick walls; metal pylons taken root like some mutant weed by the side of every road, alleyway and building to carry the new life-blood of the town to these latest beneficiaries of the electronic age; and the steel reinforcing rods which, protruding heavenwards in their thousands from the walls of almost every newly-constructed building, made the town look more like a bed of nails than a place where people actually lived. And then there was the rubbish. It was everywhere: piles of refuse, some small, some big, dumped behind buildings, in alleyways, in open spaces, in hollows and ditches; some partially buried, some partially incinerated; left for the goats, the municipality and the elements – floods, on rare occasions, and the wind that did its damnedest to scatter what it could. It seemed that in one last burst of energy in its dying years, the twentieth century had finally caught up with Tamanrasset.

It was clear to me, too, that I had picked up either the flu going around London as I left, or a chest infection. And I had forgotten how cold it could get at night; soon I was wrapping another blanket around myself. Now that I had finally arrived in the Central Sahara I had once known so well, it seemed terribly unfamiliar.

2

Meeting Bahedi

A T NINE O'CLOCK the next morning I was ready to go, standing on the pavement outside the hotel entrance, sporting dark glasses, my new 'made in Philippines' hat, and my camera bag. This was a notably positive gesture on my part, mentally speaking at least, for whatever infection had got into my chest had made its presence felt. Alternating bouts of fever and shivering had driven away sleep, and I had passed most of the night reading a heavy tome I had brought with me, about the history of Islam in Algerian politics. In Ramadan the hotel served breakfast at five, almost two hours before sunrise. I decided to put in an appearance in the dining hall, out of respect for Ramadan more than from any feelings of hunger, which seemed to have deserted me. It was freezing: I put on two sweaters and a storm jacket in an effort to counter the cold that had invaded the hotel's bleak corridors.

There was only one other person in the dining room. He looked even more disconsolate than I felt and, for want of conversation between us, I mentally labelled him a *fonctionnaire*, down from the north. The waiter brought coffee and bread and jam, and asked if I would like eggs. I said yes. I didn't feel like eggs, but I did have a sense of nutritional duty to my body and of deference to the chickens that do such sterling work in keeping scorpions under control in Saharan towns and villages.

I would have no news of Beh until the evening, so in the meantime I decided to 'beat the bounds'. The only way to get a feeling for

25

the extent and limits of this huge urban sprawl was to walk around it. By 'around', I meant literally that: I would walk the circumference. My rough calculations, based on a schoolboy memory of $2\pi r$ and an estimated radius of three kilometres, suggested a walk of about twenty kilometres, soon revised on the ground to nearer thirty.

I set off in the direction of Hadrian, the anvil-shaped mountain dominating the skyline to the east of Tamanrasset, and the little hamlet of the same name in its lee.

My progress was slow, for almost everyone I passed was keen to stop and talk. Partly this was natural curiosity, wanting to know where I was from. With tourism now virtually non-existent, people seemed genuinely pleased to see a foreigner again. I got the impression, too, that people felt a need to explain what was going on in their country. They were very ready to blame the crisis on Islamic fundamentalists.

It took me more than an hour to walk a couple of kilometres. But if my progress on the ground was slow, at least I was learning a lot from those with whom I stopped to talk. Two kilometres had taken me across the *Oued* Tamanrasset, past an empty camping site for tourists, towards a small stretch of open ground. A few hundred metres to the right I saw a vehicle graveyard. This was where the town's hundreds of old jalopies came to rest when they could no longer be held together and kept going. It was also a species of knacker's yard, where the carcasses of dozens (more likely hundreds) of vehicles that had made it thus far across the Sahara only to give up and die were dumped, after being stripped of all usable parts. A little in front of the graveyard a slight depression glinted in the sun like a pond of bright water. Closer inspection revealed a mass of broken glass, presumably from the windows of the wrecks nearby.

I had just climbed a small promontory for a better view when I heard a voice behind me. A Land Cruiser had stopped on the road and the driver was beckoning me. My stomach knotted. It must be the security police. I had been expecting a visit from them ever since checking into the hotel the previous day. As I put my camera into its case and walked slowly towards the vehicle, I had about a minute in which to think. Stay calm, I told myself. Be polite. I was in the country quite legitimately and had done nothing illegal or provocative, unless my perhaps unusual interest in the town's rubbish could be so described.

The Land Cruiser's engine was still running. As I approached the passenger window I had a good view of the single occupant. He was middle-aged, probably in his younger forties, wearing an attractive bright indigo-coloured *gandoura* or kaftan but, unusually, no *chech*. He had medium-length black, curly hair, a brown, slightly olive-coloured skin and sensitive, even refined, features. I'm not sure who said '*Bonjour*' first, but as we did so I leant through the window to shake hands. He asked me, in perfect French, where I was going.

'Nowhere in particular,' I replied, trying for a note of urbane *politesse*. 'Just out towards Hadrian.'

'Then get in,' he said. It was more invitation than command. 'I am going there myself.'

As I climbed up into the front passenger seat, my rational mind was telling me that if he wasn't a security policeman, then he must be a terrorist: I was now going to be kidnapped, or have my throat slit. But I actually *felt* no such fear or anxiety. Possibly it was his voice. It had such a soft, attractive resonance that, had I been a woman, I would surely have found it seductive. As I settled next to my putative assassin I recalled the warnings parents give their children about not accepting lifts from strangers – especially not in a crazy country like this!

'What is your name?' he asked as we pulled away.

'My name?' I repeated, wondering for a split second if there was any way of remaining anonymous. 'Jeremy Keenan.'

'I know your name,' he said. He paused to think for a moment. 'You've written a book?'

They say that your whole life flashes in front of you when you are about to drown. I've never been on the point of going down for the third time, but I think that for a second or two I felt something similar. Who *was* this man, and what else did he know about me? 'Yes,' I said. Keep it all very low-key, I thought. Don't elaborate. And then the disclaimer: 'But it was a long time ago.'

'I've heard it referred to many times, but I've never seen a copy.'

His tone seemed friendly, perhaps even complimentary; but I felt embarrassed by his reference to my book on the Tuareg, especially as I knew so little of their current situation.

'What is your name?' I asked in my turn, still uncertain whether to regard him as friend or foe.

'Mokhtar, Mokhtar Bahedi.'

I was not familiar with the name 'Bahedi', but the indigo of his dress had already led me to suspect that he was a Tuareg. 'Mokhtar ag Bahedi,' I repeated, deliberately slipping in the *ag*, which means 'son of' in Tamahak and which all Tuareg include in their names.

'Yes, that's right. But the government has got rid of *ag*.'

I wanted to ask him what the government thought it was doing, interfering with Tuareg naming, but my immediate feeling was one of relief. 'You are a Tuareg?' I hoped the note of pleasure in my voice was obvious. Then, to establish my own *bona fides*, I asked him in Tamahak, phrases of which were coming back to me, the name of his descent group (a technical usage for the Tuareg kinship affiliations, for which 'tribe' is not really either accurate or adequate).

'Kel Rezzi,' he said, having expressed surprise at my knowledge of Tamahak. I had not known the Kel Rezzi well, which was why I had not recognised his name immediately as Tuareg.

And that is how I met Mokhtar ag Bahedi, quite by chance, on the road to Hadrian.

So engrossed was I in my conversation with Bahedi that I failed to notice when we turned off the main road and passed through the village of Hadrian. We were now on the edge of open country and there were no more buildings between us and the great mountain of Hadrian except for a new mud-plastered wall about three metres or so high which appeared to surround a settlement of two or three hectares. Large metal double gates, the only entrance in the wall, stood open. As we passed through, I caught my breath. We had entered into a veritable paradise: row after row of neatly manicured raised garden beds, full of almost every vegetable one could imagine, interspersed with little orchard plots of orange trees, apricots, vines and a host of other fruits, stretched for at least a hundred metres down to the wall, beyond which was the bank of the *Oued* Tamanrasset.

'This is incredible,' I said. I could find no other word for it. 'Is it all yours?' As I spoke, I remembered that Tuareg do not like talking of their wealth or property in any way which might be interpreted as expressing either covetousness or self-satisfaction, for fear of invoking the 'evil eye'. This taboo had in the past made it almost impossible for me to discuss such points of anthropological curiosity as herd sizes, possession or ownership rights over animals, or even their general well-being.

As Bahedi nodded and looked across the gardens, I could sense his pride and affection. 'I bought it about four years ago,' he said softly, 'for a very good price.' Close to where he had stopped the Land Cruiser two men, whom he introduced as Bambara from Mali, were breaking up a large outcrop of rock with pick-axes. In the distance I could see another man at work in the gardens. I stepped down from the vehicle and was ushered through another metal gate into an inner compound. For an instant it put me in mind of a film set I had once seen in the Arizona desert, but without the cacti and the cowboys – though Bahedi himself certainly had the looks and demeanour to fit the bill. Five rooms, each designed as a separate unit, opened off a large open split-level courtyard landscaped into the contours of the natural rock. Except for two rock outcrops which provided natural seating, the courtyard was covered by immaculately clean, swept, fine gravel. On the side nearest the mountain of Hadrian, rising like a sentinel above the complex, two traditional Tuareg skin tents stood in front of a small rock garden.

'All we need now,' said Bahedi, somewhat ruefully, 'are the tourists.'

'Are there any?' I asked. I well knew that the subject of tourism was about as delicate as politics.

'We live in hope. If Bouteflika can bring an end to the troubles in the north – well ...'

'Do you think he will?' I interrupted him.

'The news is getting better. Much will depend on the ultimatum he gives to the "men in the mountains" at the end of Ramadan.'

I admired his entrepreneurial spirit. Assuredly, the future of Tamanrasset, from the Tuareg's perspective, at least, lay in its enormous potential for small-scale, select tourism. But it was a future that was being strangled by a war few people in the south could comprehend, one which was certainly winning no converts to Islamic fundamentalism.

Bahedi tried to explain to me the probable gist of Bouteflika's ultimatum to the 'terrorists' – some sort of time-limited amnesty – as he showed me through the complex: showers, toilets, kitchen, all the facilities an adventure tourist might want. The whole had been designed and built by Bahedi and his wife, whom I was yet to meet.

'We still get a few Swiss,' he said as he gestured towards the magnificent unspoilt view of the mountains of Ahaggar to the north, 'but they are mostly friends of my wife.'

So Bahedi's wife was Swiss? 'She will be back soon,' he said. 'She's fetching some stuff from the house.'

'You also have a house in town?' I tried not to sound surprised.

'Oh yes. We work here during the day, but usually spend the night in town, except when we have guests. Then we all stay here.'

I had known a few European men who had married Tuareg women. Apart from Guy Barrère who ran the school at Ideles, there was a M. Côquet, who had lived in Tamanrasset until 1968, when his wife died. I tried to think how many marriages I had known between Tuareg men and European women; certainly I had heard of a couple, but I had not met them. I was trying to put names to them in my mind when a second, older Land Cruiser drew up at the inner compound gate. 'Ah, here is Claudia,' said Bahedi.

Turning, I watched as she gathered baskets and packages from the car. A small boy, a baby image of Bahedi, scampered over to the two Bambara men, who were very ready to down tools and give him their attention. Not until she had come through the gate did Claudia see me with Bahedi. Her face broke into a huge and most welcoming smile. '*Bonjour, bonjour, comment allez-vous?*' Having assumed me to be French, she switched to perfect English as I introduced myself. Languages, as I was to discover, were just one of her many skills: she was fluent in French, English, Arabic, Tamahak and, presumably, German. Younes, aged two and a half, rushed to join us and get in on the act. He, it speedily transpired, was already trilingual in Arabic, Tamahak and French, and had picked up more than a smattering of Bambara from the migrant workers in the garden.

Claudia left to prepare us some lunch, mostly salad and fruits from her garden, which we ate on a patio area that caught the warmth of the westering sun as the three of us talked long into the afternoon.

Like Bahedi, Claudia was intrigued that I should have returned after so many years. 'It is difficult to explain,' I said. 'Suddenly I felt a need to know what has happened to the Tuareg, particularly those I knew, since I was last here.'

'Phew! Things have certainly changed,' said Claudia. 'You must have seen that as soon as you got off the plane.'

'Yes, Tamanrasset is a shock. But what about the nomads?

Yesterday, Sliman at the old Café de la Paix told me that there weren't any camps left, and that all the nomads are now settled in villages.'

'No, not entirely,' said Bahedi. He paused to think for a moment. 'It's true that most nomads are settled now. The Dag Rali, whom you would have known, are all living in villages like Terhenanet and Tagmart. Sometimes they go back into the mountains with their goats for a while if there is good pasture, but most of them are in the villages.'

'It's sad, what has become of them,' said Claudia, 'especially the women. It's becoming so degenerate.'

I wanted to follow up Claudia's remark, for this was an aspect that hadn't occurred to me, but before I could ask her to elaborate, Bahedi had broken in. 'There are still some nomads, but they are mostly far away from Tamanrasset, around the Tefedest, and to the south and east.'

'Which groups are still nomadic, and how many of them are there?'

He thought again. 'There are some Ait Lowayen, mostly Kel Tourha I think, around the Tefedest, as well as quite a few Isckkemaren. To the south and east there are some Iklan-Taoussit and Tegehe-n-Efis, and maybe a few Aguh-en-tehle to the east of Assekrem.'

It was good to hear the tribal names again. My earlier studies of the region had focused very much on the history of the many tribes and their associations. Altogether, there were at least twenty tribal groupings in Ahaggar, many traditionally consisting of no more than a few families, tied together in an amazingly complex social and political structure.

'How many of them are still nomadic – living in camps?' I asked.

We started to run through all the tribes, trying to make some sort of calculation, but it was impossible. At the best it could be no better than a guesstimate. 'Maybe three thousand,' Bahedi suggested with a shrug. 'Possibly four, but probably less – but it depends on how you define "nomad"!'

'What news of Khabte ag Abahag?' I asked. 'When I asked Sliman yesterday, he didn't seem sure, but he thought he was so old he was probably dead.'

'Khabte? You knew him?'

'I stayed with him and his family a lot, mostly when they were camped along the eastern side of the Taessa Mountains. I first met him just after he was released from prison.'

Claudia, who had been listening patiently to our tribal roll–call, interjected: 'He died less than three weeks ago. Can you believe it?'

There was a silence, as the implications of what she had said sunk in. When I last saw Khabte he was in his late sixties and not well. I had assumed that he must have died many years ago. Yet it seemed that had I returned even a month earlier, I might have seen him again. 'I have so many memories of Khabte,' I said. 'It may sound a bit silly, but in many ways I always thought of him as the "last nomad". Maybe it was just because I knew him so well, but he seemed to sym-bolise everything that had happened to the Tuareg since before the French came.' I felt immensely sad, as if something very profound had been taken from the land.

'I don't think that's silly,' said Claudia. 'He spent much of his life as a young boy in Tamesna, down in Niger, looking after camels. And he was quite a man; he had more pride than most of the others. He never took hand-outs.'

I tried to calculate how old he must have been when he died. I made it ninety-two or ninety-three.

'His family say ninety-eight,' Claudia offered. I was not going to argue the toss; anything over ninety was a good age, and anyway I knew enough of Tuareg chronologies to be aware that precision was probably unattainable. The years of the Tuareg calendar are named after such significant events as raids, good rains, or drought. Recorded in memory and folklore, not writing, they become a little sketchy over time.

'And how are his family?'

'You remember his wife, Tebubirt?'

'Yes. She was a beautiful woman.'

'They say she was the beauty of her day.'

'Like Dassine,' I said, 'when the French first arrived here.' Dassine was a noblewoman of great beauty and – according to Charles de Foucauld, the French priest who lived among the Tuareg at the beginning of the twentieth century – of immense intelligence, who exerted considerable influence on affairs of state. Her beauty was renowned throughout the region, and even after her marriage she was courted by many nobles, including the Amenukal, the para-mount chief, Moussa ag Amastene, who had led the Kel Ahaggar in their defence against the French. Dassine repeatedly rejected Moussa's proposals, on the grounds that he was ugly. Moussa was allegedly so humiliated by this that he refused to touch another Tuareg woman and instead took two slave-girls as wives. Such was the vanity of Ahaggar's great nobles that when Dassine walked out on her husband, Bouhen, he likewise turned to slave-girls.

'Yes, I suppose she was a bit like Dassine: the *belle* of her age. She's in seclusion now.' Claudia explained: 'I expect you remember that she cannot see anyone for three months, now. The last time I saw her, a few months before Khabte's death, she was well. Remember, she's at least twenty years younger than Khabte. As for the sons, Abdullah is working in Mali and only seems to come home once a year – to keep his new wife pregnant! El Boghari – well, he's married again too, to another cousin I believe, and living in Tagmart.'

Abdullah must have been approaching fifty and El Boghari about forty. When he was a boy of about ten, I used to help El Boghari collect wood for the camp. Every two or three days we would go clambering into the gorges of the Tacssa in search of firewood. Abdullah I had met for the first time about two weeks after his marriage, and that was shortly after his return from his first caravan to Niger – perhaps the biggest event in a young man's life, apart from marriage. I well remembered the scenes in the camp, and especially I remembered Abdullah's eyes. They were the replica of his mother's.

'Did you know that Abdullah's first wife died?' Claudia asked.

'No,' I said. 'But I have had no news at all since I was last here. What happened to her?'

'I don't know the details, but she was ill.'

We talked, and we talked. We reminisced about Khabte's life and his family, and Bahedi did his best to fill me in on what had been happening in the camps and mountains during my long absence. We talked incessantly, like long-lost brothers with thirty years of news to catch up on.

Finally, with the sun about to set, Bahedi reminded me that I was to meet Sliman that evening. He offered to drive me back into Tamanrasset, but I was reluctant to impose on him. I assured him I was more than happy to walk. Before we could overwhelm one another with politeness, Claudia came up with a suggestion: I must borrow her bicycle.

'I couldn't do that,' I said. I didn't want to inconvenience her – but more than that, I couldn't remember when I had last ridden a bike.

'But I have two, and one I hardly ever use. You could borrow it while you're here, as long as you don't mind it being a lady's.' I had a fleeting premonition of what she was going to say: 'Do you remember a Miss Jackson?'

Miss Jackson had been governess to an English missionary family who were living in Tamanrasset when I first arrived there but soon moved south to Niger. One of my first memories of Tamanrasset was of Miss Jackson riding sedately into the little town, skirts billowing, straight-backed and red-cheeked. She never once spoke to me.

'Don't tell me it's *her* bike!' I laughed.

'Yes, it is hers, and it's probably about the same age she was!'

And there it stood, with its wide, old-fashioned saddle and shopping basket, still in good working order. I had some trouble keeping my balance over the sand, but by the time I reached the tarmac road I had the hang of it.

I have crossed large stretches of the Sahara on foot, with donkeys, on camel and, of course, in various vehicles; but this was something entirely new to me. Lawrence of Arabia's ride down the Wadi Rum into Akaba may have been something of a cinematic *tour de force*, but my ride into Tamanrasset on a bicycle nearly my own age that had once belonged to an English missionary's governess was also something to behold. I felt exhilarated after my day with Bahedi, and as if in celebration I pedalled faster and faster, crashing through the gears as I rode triumphantly into the setting sun. Lawrence had nothing on this – eat your heart out, David Lean! Fortunately, the town was at prayer, and the streets were temporarily deserted.

3

In search of Mokhtar

IT WAS AFTER ten in the morning before we had finally loaded the
Land Cruiser, bought bread and a few other last-minute items, and
set off on the main road north from Tamanrasset, heading for the
Tefedest Mountains, the second biggest range in Ahaggar.

Our driver Hosseyni took the wheel – also a Kel Rezzi, though
no relation, he occasionally worked for Bahedi – with Bahedi in
the front passenger seat. I sat in the back, a position I had deliberately chosen with the idea that it might afford me just a fraction
more protection in the event of a collision with one of the local
speed-merchants. Hosseyni proved to be a good driver, though,
especially when he got off the *piste* and had to thread his way over
the rough desert surface. A strapping young man of about twenty-
eight, married with two young children, he still exuded the physical fitness that I presumed he had honed during his military service.
Leaving urban life behind them and setting their faces towards the
desert, Bahedi and Hosseyni wore the Tuareg veil, Bahedi with his
usual indigo *gandoura*, Hosseyni with a shirt, jacket and jeans. I was
less than picturesque, in shirt and trousers and without a headcloth.

Planning the trip – or, to be more exact, deciding where in
Ahaggar I would go – had not been an easy matter. I had spent the
best part of a week deliberating with Bahedi about where I might
find nomadic Tuareg. By 'nomadic' I meant Tuareg who still lived in
tents, rather than reed huts or mud-brick houses in cultivation

centres, and whose primary activity was tending their camels and goat herds. Yet 'nomadic' has always been something of a misnomer. Even in traditional, pre-colonial times the Tuareg were more semi-nomadic than nomadic, moving their camps within relatively circumscribed areas for the most part, depending on the state and availability of pasture.

In spite of what I had heard in London and from people like Sliman in Tamanrasset about the Kel Ahaggar being now all settled, both Bahedi and Beh, themselves Tuareg, had reassured me: the nomadic life had not been entirely abandoned, and some Kel Ahaggar, if perhaps not more than a few hundred, were still living in semi-nomadic camps. I wanted to find them, spend some time with them, and discover if I could how much remained of their traditional existence, way of life and values.

Catching up with Beh had not after all been as simple as Sliman's suggestion of dinner had presupposed, though Sliman had his telephone number. This I found both hilarious and incongruous. Most Tuareg men are so completely veiled that nothing is visible of their faces except a slit around the eyes. Even for eating or drinking the veil is not lowered, food being passed to the mouth beneath it. Using a telephone must of course have been easier than that, but the idea was somehow so irresistably comic that I longed for a cartoonist's skill. I rang Beh several times, both from the hotel and from Bahedi's house, but to no avail. Whether the blame lay with Ramadan or the basic technology I don't know, but the Tamanrasset phones seemed to be out of order for most of the time I was there; when they did work, wrong numbers were about all I could get.

Happily, however, even in a town the size of Tamanrasset it is not difficult to track down one particular Tuareg. They number only a few thousand, and if they do not know one another directly, as kinsmen, they know *of* one another, by tribal association and hearsay. Sliman knew roughly where Beh lived, and with Bahedi's help I soon found his home. I felt strangely nervous at the prospect of seeing him again after so many years.

Bahedi knocked on Beh's door. As we waited, I wondered if I would recognise him. I remembered him as a lean six-footer, nearly always dressed, at least day-to-day, in a slightly flecked, sky-blue-coloured *gandoura* and *chech*. Like all Tuareg of noble descent, Beh expressed the haughtiness of his breeding in his demeanour and deportment. In the past, I used to sit in the Café de la Paix in the evenings and watch Tuareg strolling down the main street. The nobles were always instantly recognisable from their carriage and style of dress. Beh, I remembered, had always had a reputation for elegance.

The door was opened by a young girl, presumably one of Beh's daughters. Beh himself was standing just behind her, looking so extraordinary that for a second I almost did not recognise him. He was wearing a pure white, immaculately creased *gandoura* and a pure white *tagelmoust*, the Tuareg's own word for the veil the Arabs call a *chech*. He might have been fashioned from icing sugar, or *blanc de chine* porcelain.

'*Monsieur Keenan, bonjour*,' said the soft, languid voice I remembered so well. 'Sliman told me you were back in town.' Rather than simply shaking my hand he clasped it in both of his, and without letting go led me into his front room. Its floor was of coarse sand and there was no furniture except for some brightly coloured blankets and cushions arranged by another of his daughters. Beh's veil was worn just about at its highest, but through the narrow slit I could see enough of his eyes to know that he was smiling broadly. I felt like throwing my arms around him in a huge hug – but by holding my hand and revealing his smile in his eyes, he was already expressing more emotion than was becoming in a noble.

Bahedi left us after a few words with Beh, which I did not hear. We would meet again later.

Sliman had told me Beh had remarried since I left and had several more children, but he was not sure how many. 'Seven,' said Beh proudly, after he had introduced me to his wife. She looked remarkably young, though she must I thought have been at least forty. Beh himself was approaching seventy, and I had been anxious lest he too might have died before my return. As it was, he looked fitter and more full of bounce than I had ever known him, clearly invigorated by remarriage after several years of lonely widowhood, and another clutch of children.

We sat and talked for almost two hours. Repeatedly he asked me how I was, how many children I had now that I was married, how much I remembered of what he had taught me as my *professeur*. It was a strange conversation, in that we talked about surprisingly little apart from our respective families and our health. Possibly it was because his French had deteriorated, as had my Tamahak. But I felt it was more because our family circumstances were now so different, and because we were both so much older. We were now 'the older generation' and had taken on its mantle. Whenever I asked Beh for news of the region generally, the conversation soon reverted to reminiscences of our previous times together. On this first and somewhat emotionally charged occasion, at least, it seemed that we were locked in the past. While we talked Beh made tea, and another of his daughters brought me a plate of fresh *baguette* and a full box of processed cheese. Beh did not join me, because of Ramadan, but insisted that I eat every last morsel of cheese. One still needed strong guts, I realised, to survive the hospitality of the desert, even in town.

When I left, it occurred to me how strange it was that in more than thirty years I had never seen Beh's face. I had recognised him solely by the style of his dress, notably his veil, and, as soon as he spoke, by his voice. He was still the most elegant Tuareg I had ever met. As Bahedi jokingly put it when I saw him later, he would without a doubt win Tamanrasset's 'best-dressed man' award.

I had chosen Tefedest in part because the Ait Lowayen who live there were particularly interesting to me for various reasons, and in part because Bahedi had good contacts with a number of Ait Lowayen groups and thought we would be able to find them without too much difficulty. Additionally, Tefedest is in many ways the most beautiful range of mountains in Ahaggar. Without doubt Atakor, the high central mountain area of Ahaggar, with its great extinct volcanoes and volcanic plugs, is the most dramatic in the region, perhaps in the whole of North Africa, but for me at least Tefedest, a hundred and sixty kilometres or so north of Atakor, is more subtle in its magnificence. The ballooned, heavily-weathered granites, the deep valleys and surrounding acacia-covered plains are more African than Saharan.

My particular reasons for wanting to journey through the Tefedest mountains were however a little less straightforward than a mere appreciation of superlative scenery. One could be described as 'unfinished' business; the other was, I had a feeling, more in the nature of business about to begin.

The 'unfinished business' concerned France's nuclear testing programme: in 1962 France had exploded her first nuclear device under the mountain at In Eker, about eighty kilometres due west of the little cultivation centre of Mertoutek at the southern end of the Tefedest.

Soon after my first visit to Ahaggar, I began to hear rumours of an accident during the 1962 explosion at In Eker. A portal on the east side of the mountain under which the device had been detonated was said to have blown open, a cloud of radioactivity had escaped, and the military observers had run for their vehicles, the generals getting there first and leaving the soldiers behind. No doubt the story was over-dramatised in the telling, yet I believe a small number of French soldiers did in fact die.

I thought little more about these stories until 1969, by which time the French had departed from In Eker. In that year I learned from a young, very intelligent doctor stationed briefly in Tamanrasset of six or seven young children who had been brought into the Tamanrasset hospital over a six-month period suffering from diarrhoea and associated stomach disorders. All had died. For religious reasons he had been unable to perform full autopsies, but the doctor was of the opinion that all the children were suffering from some form of stomach or intestinal tumour. Their ages suggested to me that all had probably been in the womb at the time of the In Eker bomb test, a connection that supported the doctor's analysis.

A sense of outrage had prompted me to write to the press, in the hope of drawing attention to what might have happened at In Eker. My letter was published, but elicited no response. Perhaps that was not surprising: it was now several years after the incident, and the Cold War was at its height. It was a time when the prevailing public feeling in the West was that such sacrifices – especially if they occurred in far-off places – were the inevitable price of progress and security.

The incident had continued to bother me over the years, and not just because it involved the death of children. My conscience nagged me: I was possibly the only person to be aware of this small fragment of evidence, inconclusive though it obviously was.

I asked Bahedi whether he recalled the In Eker bomb explosion.

'I was only five or six years old at the time. We were living in Tamanrasset, but I can still remember the "bang". All the doors and windows shook. And I can still remember people talking about it.'

'What about the Tefedest and Mertoutek?' I asked.

'Something serious certainly happened there. Claudia and I have both heard stories of many animals dying, and of people being taken ill and dying after the "bang". One of the strangest things is that for many years a number of plants and vegetables failed to grow. It is only recently, in the last few years, so some people say, that some species have begun to grow again in the area.'

'Whatever happened was some forty years ago and beyond most people's memories,' I said. 'If I am to find out what happened, I'll need to talk with the old people.'

'There are still plenty who will be able to remember,' Bahedi assured me. 'It will just be a matter of getting them to think clearly. The problem is that few of them understood what was going on at In Eker, or the dangers of radioactivity.'

My second particular reason for wanting to visit the Tefedest had to do with the prehistoric rock art to be found there. The mountains of the Central Sahara are rich in prehistoric rock paintings and engravings, dating back some twelve thousand years to a time when the Sahara was much wetter.

Before leaving London I had come across a news report of terrorist activity in south-east Algeria, but it made no specific reference to either the location, or the nature of the incidents. In the course of an Internet search in which I keyed in the names of almost everywhere I could think of in the Central Sahara on the off-chance of finding a report which might clarify what was happening there, I turned up an article published on the BBC's website about Libyan tourism. It had been written in May 1998, and its author, Jonathan Fryer, had been visiting the Acacus mountains near Ghat, a small town in southern Libya close to the Algerian border. His penultimate paragraph read:

'The walls of one cave depict the preparations and ceremonials for a wedding – or did. For as the Touareg guide explained, since he was last there, only a year before, half of them had gone. Some had clearly been chipped off the rock as souvenirs. Others had simply been washed away, by people throwing water at them, to heighten their colour for photographs.'

As I read this paragraph, the thought crossed my mind that if cave paintings were being hacked out of the Acacus mountains in Libya, it was likely that the thieves would also have visited the much richer and better-known Tassili sites in Algeria. The Tassili-n-Ajjer lies to the north-east of Ahaggar and is quite easy to get to from Libya. If rock art thieves had entered the Tassili, then perhaps they had ventured as deep into Algeria as the Tefedest. The rock art there is not as well-known as that of the Tassili, but probably just as attractive to a private collector or the commercial market, if that was for whom it was being plundered.

I was already planning to undertake a search of the main Tassili sites after my journey through the Tefedest: if rock art was being stolen, as I suspected, it would be sensible to check out the Tefedest sites as well, while I was in the region.

My plans for finding the Ait Lowayen and travelling through the Tefedest seemed to me haphazard in the extreme. As there had been no means of contacting any of the Ait Lowayen before leaving Tamanrasset, there was no guarantee that they would be able to accompany me, or even that camels or other forms of transport would be available. But Bahedi was more confident. His plan was to drive as far as the *Oued* Mertoutek at the southern end of the Tefedest, and there make contact with Mokhtar ag Mohammed, whom he knew well and who, I gathered, was the head of this small section of the Kel Tourha Ait Lowayen.

(Mokhtar ag Bahedi and Mokhtar ag Mohammed are not related: the fact that they share the same name is merely a coincidence, and a slightly inconvenient one. To avoid confusion I have been referring to Mokhtar ag Bahedi as 'Bahedi'. Mokhtar ag Mohammed will be known as 'Mokhtar'. To complicate matters further, I learned later of yet another Mokhtar, a certain Mokhtar ben Mokhtar – but him I shall leave aside until he enters the story.)

As we set off from Tamanrasset, then, our immediate objective was to find Mokhtar. According to Bahedi, he was camped out somewhere in the *Oued* Mertoutek, and he would have camels with which I would be able to travel through the Tefedest.

We hadn't gone far into the open desert beyond the airport junction on the main road north from Tamanrasset when we came across a huge complex of what looked like modern warehouses, spreading a kilometre or so up the valley to our right. For a split second I assumed it to be some sort of factory, until I noticed the pill-box sentry lookouts perched at regular intervals on the high walls.

'Otoul,' said Bahedi.

'Is that a prison?' I asked, aware that the Algerian government often found it convenient to use the Sahara for this purpose.

It was Hosseyni who replied: 'No, it's an army barracks – a supply depot, I believe. There are two more, just as big, a bit further up the road at Tit.'

Otoul, as I remembered it, had contained nothing but a well, a few gardens and a small community of slaves who had once worked the gardens for their Tuareg masters. Looking at it again now, it seemed curious that such an apparently insignificant little settlement should have been the focus of the stories which spread across the Sahara in the summer of 1964, that the Tuareg had taken up arms against the newly independent Algerian government. On their return from a six-month caravan to Niger, five local Dag Rali Tuareg had taken it upon themselves to ride on Otoul to reclaim their former slaves. Fortunately for all concerned, the resulting skirmish merely took the form of a slanging match; the ex-slaves sought cover behind boulders, and no one was killed. The only serious injury was to one of the Tuareg, who was shot in the foot when his musket went off accidentally. The five Tuareg were given three-year gaol sentences, and after their release I got to know them all, none better than their supposed ringleader, Khabte ag Abahag. There was a certain pathos in the sight of a huge military barracks where the Tuareg had made what was probably their last, albeit futile and misguided, attempt to re-establish their former rights and supremacy.

I looked up the valley, wondering what remained of the old slave village, its well and gardens. It struck me as extraordinarily poignant that I should be passing by Otoul again only two or three weeks after the death of Khabte ag Abahag. Bizarrely enough, Khabte had in fact lived his last few years about fifteen kilometres further up the *oued*, at the little Dag Rali village of Tagmart. Beyond Tagmart, rising high in front of us and to our right, were the great mountains of Atakor in which the Dag Rali tribesmen had lived in their nomadic camps since time immemorial. Each in its own way, the military barracks and Khabte's death, were sadly symbolic of the end of an era in which the nomad had reigned supreme.

Twenty kilometres further up the road we passed the village of Tit. Since it is the Berber word for 'spring' or 'source', there are dozens of places in North Africa called Tit. In Tamanrasset I once met a very confused Englishwoman who had been inspired to travel to Algeria after reading this epithet at the end of a chapter in a book by J.P. Donleavy: 'In Algeria there is a village called Tit.' In search of Donleavy's Tit, she had wanted to know if this particular village might be it. I couldn't help her: I looked through Donleavy's book (I have forgotten the title), but found no other reference to Algeria.

Once consisting of a few huts by the old dirt road and some well-watered gardens further down the *oued*, Tit was now a military zone with two massive depots taking up much of the valley. Again, the military presence was strangely symbolic, for it was around a small boulder-strewn hillock about three kilometres further down the *oued* that the Tuareg were finally defeated by the French in 1902.

With a hundred voluntarily enlisted *méharistes* from the Tidikelt, Lieutenant Cottenest had left In Salah to make a reconnaissance of Ahaggar and inflict a punitive raid on the Kel Ahaggar. As the patrol travelled through the Mouydir (Immidir) and Tefedest mountains to Ideles, then around the east of Atakor to Tamanrasset before returning northwards, they were watched by the Kel Ahaggar, who no doubt remembered the ease with which, some twenty years earlier, they had destroyed a slightly smaller French column. Finally, at this most ill-judged of places, the Kel Ahaggar launched a furious attack on the patrol. Although they rallied courageously, successive assaults withered in the face of the accurate fire from the French positioned behind that easily-defended hillock.

We walked around the base of the hillock for a few minutes. Bahedi and Hosseyni both lit cigarettes. It was a cruel place for such a

battle: the hillock, which looks more like a huge pile of boulders surrounded by a flat rocky plain, could have been held by a handful of
men against an entire army.

The inscription on a monument erected beside the hillock said
that seventy-two Tuareg had been killed, and that their remains had
subsequently been removed and reburied in Tamanrasset. The histor-
ical records say Cottenest lost three dead, with ten injured, and I had
always understood that more than a hundred Kel Ahaggar had been
killed. But whatever the precise number, it was here, at this desolate
spot, that the Kel Ahaggar's territorial sovereignty had been shat-
tered, along with their notions of their own invincibility.

We climbed back into the Land Cruiser and drove off. No one
spoke. I wondered what Bahedi and Hosseyni were thinking. My
own mind was wandering among battle sites visited in other parts of
the world, where other once-proud people had fallen to the superior
fire-power of colonial overlords.

As we continued northwards, the desert seemed more parched and
arid than I had remembered it. There had been no rain at all for
almost four months, according to Bahedi, and pasturage was meagre.
I looked up at the great mountains of Atakor on our right, the volcanoes of Tahat, Ilaman and Amjer and the almost impenetrable jungle
of pink granite that made up the mountain range of Taessa, once the
home of the Dag Rali. There, high above us, fresh, running water
was to be found in the many, often deeply hidden, *gueltas* (water-
holes), and with it hundreds of plant species, some lethal, some
medicinal or simply aromatic, and many so small, discreet and tucked
away that only a trained eye could see them. In the high mountains of
Atakor, as in the Tefedest, the beauty of nature is infinite, and at its
most microcosmic.

Soon the horizon ahead of us became filled by the bulbous presence of In Eker's mountain, standing isolated, as if shunned by other
mountains for what it had done. The death-like silver-grey of its
huge, flaking granite slabs, peeling off its smooth, domed surface like
the layers of an onion, was like cold steel in the glare of the sun. I
wondered how many people this mountain had killed, and how
much had been covered up. The military records are still closed, and
will probably remain so for a very long time.

I wanted to continue right up to the old atomic base at In Eker, so
that I could photograph its evil face at close range; but we were

running behind time, and our turn-off to the east was about forty kilometres south of it.

The road we turned onto was the *piste* running due east to the villages of Hirafok and Ideles and then on for another five hundred kilometres to Djanet and the Tassili. Then we left the Hirafok *piste*, and instead of taking the recognised *piste* to Mertoutek Hosseyni struck out directly across the desert towards the Tefedest. Occasionally we seemed to be following some sort of track, but for much of the time we were in four-wheel drive, climbing up and down the banks of *oueds* and crawling over broken rock terrain at a walking pace. Hosseyni seemed to be following the *oueds* as much as possible; their fairly compact, sandy beds offered a good passage. But before long I could tell that in fact he was following his nose or, to be a little more exact, the other vehicle tracks that could be seen heading up almost every single *oued* and tributary. We would follow a *oued*, then probe into its tributaries looking for a passage that looked as though it would take us over the water-shed ridges of the gently undulating plain and into the next *oued* system, where the whole process would start all over again. In this crab-like advance to the Tefedest we passed through a dozen *oued* systems at least, not a single one without vehicle tracks in it. Even I could tell that not all of them led to Mertoutek.

I asked Bahedi and Hosseyni why there were so many tracks. There was an almost imperceptible hesitation, then: 'They were probably made by hunters.' We had it was true seen three gazelles, but to hunt a gazelle from a vehicle involves driving at quite high speeds, with frequent changes of direction, of which these tracks showed no signs. When I remarked on this to Bahedi, he suggested carelessly that perhaps they belonged instead to *contrabandiers*. That, I thought, was much more likely. Before leaving London I had heard that contraband, especially such things as cigarettes, was big business across the Sahara, and that Algeria was the primary market.

It took us a further four hours to reach the southern end of the Tefedest, by which time night had fallen. No sooner had we found the track leading through the mountains to the little village of Mertoutek than Hosseyni left it in search of Mokhtar's camp, swinging the Land Cruiser into the sandy bed of the *Oued* Mertoutek. In the dark it was difficult to see where we were going. The valley appeared to be tightly boxed in by the mountains rising sharply on either side, their tops silhouetted high above us as the night squeezed the last glimmers of twilight out of the valley. Hosseyni drove in a series of figures-of-eight, raking his headlights back and forth along both banks in his search for Mokhtar, a task made even more difficult by the forest of tamarisks crowding the valley floor. At times their feathery branches reduced our vision to a matter of metres. We threaded back and forth across the valley for at least half an hour, the wheels sinking in *fesh-fesh* (soft sand) every few minutes, when we would have to grind out with all four wheels engaged in bottom gear. Every few minutes Hosseyni stopped and climbed a short way up the valley side, looking for signs of a campfire. Finally, after we had traversed several kilometres of the valley floor in this way, and without any forewarning, we came out of a cluster of tamarisks and probably would have driven over the tent if we had been going much faster. Stopping a few metres short of it, Hosseyni left the engine running while he and Bahedi, adjusting their veils, went to speak with whoever might be there.

I sat where I was, watching the grossly distorted shadows of their movements and gesticulations thrown onto the backdrop of tamarisks by the headlights. Something seemed to be amiss. After a few minutes Bahedi and Hosseyni returned, followed by a one-legged young man on crutches and clutching a blanket, his face unveiled. Moving with extraordinary speed and dexterity, he opened the rear door and climbed in beside me without assistance. I took his crutches and laid them on top of the petrol and water jerricans behind us. By way of greeting, he gave me one of the widest and most beautiful smiles I have ever seen. His name was Bouiya, he was eighteen, and he was Mokhtar's second son.

From the intense conversation between Bahedi, Hosseyni and Bouiya which followed, I gathered that Mokhtar was camped out elsewhere, perhaps anything between fifteen and twenty-five kilometres further down the *oued*. This was his main camp, but only his frail wife Baha was here, with Bouiya and Mokhtar's young daughter. Mokhtar and his youngest son had taken the goats some way down the valley in search of pasture. Bouiya knew only the general direction in which his father might be, so off we went on another search, this time down the *Oued* Mertoutek and up every tributary that came into it. Finally, after an hour of intensive hunting through a seemingly endless forest of tamarisks and sandy-bottomed *oueds*, we found the makeshift camp. There was no tent. Mokhtar had built a temporary shelter of sticks and branches, little more than a windbreak, around the gnarled and twisted trunk of an old tamarisk.

Greetings were exchanged with each of us in turn, the soft touch of the palm, accompanied by the almost ritual expression of concern, in a mixture of Tamahak and Arabic, for the other's good health and welfare, peace and praise to God: *Labes – Selam er'ley-koum – Ma t toulid?* (Reply: *Elkîr r'âs*) – *Slermum – Ilhamdu lillaah* ... Even in the darkness, I could sense that Mokhtar was excited by our visit.

We squeezed into the shelter, seating ourselves on the few blankets that were all Mokhtar possessed in the way of 'furniture' with our feet close to the embers of the small fire as Mokhtar began the complex ritual of tea-making, with the two tiny teapots and the thimble-sized glasses, and all the graceful, stylised gestures I recalled so vividly. The darkness, lit by little more than the glow of the embers, made it difficult for me to see Mokhtar, except occasionally when he placed a fresh piece of wood on the embers and fanned them back into life. The flames then danced around the hearth just long enough for me to glimpse what little of his face his veil left exposed. Each flare of light threw up different angles and perspectives, and more and more I was reminded of Khabte. As is customary for a man of age and seniority (from what I could see of his face, hands and feet, I put him in his late fifties or early sixties), his veil was worn lower and more casually than either Bahedi's or Hosseyni's, exposing not just his eyes but the upper part of his cheeks, most of his nose and, every so often, when he let it fall, his mouth. The flecks of grey in his scant facial hair and his hawkish eyes and nose were very reminiscent of Khabte, and his slight build was the same. I had no doubt that he was just as wiry and tough. Mokhtar was aglow with energy and animation at having unexpected guests. His sharp eyes, watering a little from the smoke of the fire or perhaps from old age, darted back and forth, taking in each of us in turn as the conversation followed the pattern I remembered so well: slow, drawing out news of people, pasture, camels, Tamanrasset; and then the leisurely recapitulation. Here, in this far-off corner of the Sahara, time was the servant of such precious human contact and conversation. As I sat huddled by the fire, thirty years might never have passed. Khabte was here, sitting in front of me; only his name and his kinsmen had changed. The texture of the blankets, the smell of the smouldering acacia wood, mixed with that of the goats which inched their way ever closer to the warmth of human bodies, blankets and fire, were just as I remembered them.

Bahedi and I sat inside the shelter, Mokhtar at its entrance. Hosseyni, having unloaded provisions from the Land Cruiser, sat a little behind him, preparing our evening meal. I wondered what Mokhtar would have eaten if we had not turned up. There was no sign of food in the shelter. Bouiya sat on my right, still smiling, as if simply being alive was something to celebrate. Beyond him, at the edge of the shelter, his younger brother and another young boy (I later learned he was a Kel Aïr herdboy from Niger), both dressed in the flimsiest of *gandouras*, sat in silent observation of the men from Tamanrasset, every so often casting a discreet glance in my direction. By the light of the fire I could see that Bouiya's leg had been taken off just below the knee. Was it the result of illness, or an accident? His younger brother had made sure that his crutches were placed close behind him.

It was a while before Mokhtar spoke directly to me. Busy with the tea, initially he conversed predominantly with Bahedi. Bahedi explained what I was planning, and why we had thus dropped in on him, completely out of the blue. He also told Mokhtar, rather misleadingly, that I spoke Tamahak. When Mokhtar first addressed me, therefore, it was in his own language rather than in French, of which he had a smattering, to confirm this surprising information.

One of my biggest problems with the language was that I had perforce acquired a lot of rather esoteric terminology – the words for all the subtle kinship ties, the names of poisonous, aromatic and medicinal herbs, technical terms relating to camels and goats, and so forth – all once necessary for the purposes of my anthropological studies. To ask whether *efelehleh*, a most dangerous herb with a prominent place in Tuareg history, or perhaps *tehergelé*, an aromatic herb, were to be found locally, was to invite the assumption that my familiarity with such arcana reflected a very much more profound knowledge of Tamahak than I possessed. Even thirty years before, each time I asked such technical questions, I had known I was letting myself in for trouble. But Tuareg so rarely meet a European with any knowledge at all of Tamahak that they are always delighted to encounter one who is familiar with at least the basics of their language. When I replied to Mokhtar, in my best Tamahak, that I could now speak it only a little, because it was such a long time since I was last here, he let out a high-pitched whoop – '*Issan tamahak!* He knows Tamahak!' – and promptly gripped my forearm as if I were a long-lost friend.

'Do you want to see paintings, or meet people?' he asked me, when I had repeated what Bahedi had already told him about my reasons for returning to Ahaggar and coming to the Tefedest. I had not thought of it as an 'either–or' situation, but quickly saw the drift of his thinking. When we had dropped in so totally unexpectedly on his tiny makeshift camp in this far-off corner of Ahaggar, it must have seemed to him as though a pot of gold had dropped into his lap. While 'paintings' meant a lonely trek through the mountains, 'people' meant visiting all his kinsmen and friends – in short, a paid and very social holiday! I say 'paid' because Bahedi and I had made it clear that I would pay him the standard rate for both his services as a guide and the rent of his camels. From what I could gather, neither Mokhtar nor I think any other Tuareg in the area had worked as a 'guide' since the outbreak of Algeria's troubles in 1992. Taking me around the camps in this way would justify Mokhtar's recently-acquired status as a 'Gardien du Parc' and enhance his influence with tourist agencies in Tamanrasset.

'What I would really like to do,' I said, 'is meet as many Ait Lowayen as possible, as well as any other nomads who might be in the region. But I would also like to visit as many of the rock art sites as possible while I'm here.' It was obvious that this was music to his ears: he wanted an excuse to visit his chums. The trip would be a glorious social occasion, and he would be able to dine out on it for some time to come.

Until late into the night we sat huddled around the fire, exchanging news and information. Mokhtar welcomed what was for him a rare treat, that of adult companionship. It struck me that, at least superficially, not much had changed since I was last in a Tuareg camp. Mokhtar's little shelter could have been any of a number of such hearths I had sat around in years gone by. Nor had the conversation changed much. Mokhtar was happily doing most of the talking. Watching him, listening to his exuberant high-pitched voice, reminded me of my first night in Khabte's camp. That was in 1968, shortly after his release from gaol. It was late summer, and it had been raining on and off, sometimes quite heavily, for most of the day. Rather than welcoming the rain for the fresh pasture it would bring, Khabte had spent most of the day huddled under a blanket, convinced he was about to succumb to the *grippe*. As darkness fell the goats, apparently sharing his miserable outlook, sought shelter in the tent. For a while his wife Tebubirt and I shooed them out again, but after a couple of hours we gave up and their persistence prevailed. They clambered all over us, two or three deep, in their efforts to get out of the rain. I lay crushed against the ground by their weight, almost retching from their stench but grateful for their warmth, and vaguely aware that they were not fussy about where they urinated.

Now, as I sat shivering in the cold night air, looking at Mokhtar's eyes and thinking how much they resembled Khabte's, I became aware of two kids, probably no more than a month old, which had crept through the sticks behind me and were doing their best to nuzzle under my jacket. For reasons I cannot explain, their smell no longer bothered me. In fact, I found their presence almost comforting. It was as if we – humans and goats – were all in the same boat together. On my other side, Bouiya and his younger brother sat with their knees drawn up, arms clasped tightly around them, sharing what warmth a single blanket provided.

If Bahedi had not made a move, Mokhtar would probably have sat talking all night. From the vehicle Bahedi and Hosseyni took two piles of blankets which they laid on the ground by either front wheel. I had a tent, but didn't feel like trying to put it up on this first night out in the desert, in the dark. Instead, I laid out my own sleeping bag on the hard, compact sand, its top next to the rear wheel, hoping for a modicum of shelter from the wind. To protect it from freezing night air I then wrapped my head in the five metres of cotton cloth I had bought in Tamanrasset to use as a *chech*, and crawled inside. It was a long time since I had last used a sleeping bag. This one was 'top of the range', designed for Everest conditions, with a triple zip system and a price-tag to match. It was the first time I had so much as unrolled it, but I had total confidence in its ability to restore and maintain my body heat. The ground was hard, but not uncomfortably so. That was not why I lay awake for a long time. There was just enough of a gap around my eyes to let me scan the myriad stars that belong to desert nights. As my body warmed up I began to relax, and to appreciate their matchless beauty, beauty that was magnified by the enormity of the silence over which they presided. As I lay there I thought of many hundreds of other nights spent lying on the open ground of Ahaggar in just such circumstances. As my memory brought them back to me, and with them details of the journeys of which they were a part, I felt an increasing confidence, both in myself and about being where I was. There was but one remaining anxiety: tomorrow I would have to learn to mount and ride a camel all over again.

4

Tefedest
of railways and bombs

I SLEPT FITFULLY, waking several times before daylight, each time becoming rudely conscious of the freezing night air and rapidly withdrawing my head, tortoise-like, into the protection of my sleeping bag. One consolation of the bitterly cold nights of this time of year is that they force the horned viper (*cerastes*) so common in this part of the Sahara to spend several months in hibernation. When first I came to Ahaggar it was summer, and one of the first things I had to learn was to be careful about where I slept on the ground at night. Now, in midwinter, I could at least be fairly sure I would not find one of those deadly little reptiles cuddled up to me for warmth during the night.

It was getting on for eight o'clock before the sun had begun to take the chill out of the air. Neither Bahedi nor Hosseyni was yet astir as I surveyed my surroundings from the comfort of my sleeping bag. A scene of immense tranquillity was heightened, as such scenes often are in the desert, by the brightness and clarity of the light. Mokhtar was awake, sitting alone by the hearth in the shelter he had made against the roots and fallen branches of the big old tamarisk tree. He was swathed in blankets, with his veil almost off his face.

Much has been written on the subject of the Tuareg veil, and why it is that Tuareg men, not women, wear it. The Tuareg's *tagelmoust* is the one thing that above all else symbolises 'being a Tuareg'. As several

53

writers have suggested, it is indeed some protection against the sun, wind and sand, but its key function is social. The Tuareg deem it shameful for a man to expose his mouth, especially before women, parents-in-law, elders and other respected persons. Tuareg have a saying that the veil and trousers are brothers, the relationship between the two garments being that they both cover external orifices. As these orifices are considered 'zones of pollution', it is therefore extremely disrespectful to expose them before others. Traditionally, and certainly when I was with the Tuareg thirty years ago, the veil was rarely taken off, and only persons of the highest and lowest status might allow it to fall below the mouth. Only a Hadj, someone who has made the pilgrimage to Mecca, could divest himself entirely of the veil, and this suggests a sacred element to the beliefs surrounding it.

Thirty years ago many Tuareg, especially the older ones, still believed that internal illnesses were attributable to evil spirits, the Kel Asouf, and that the veil protected against their entry into the body. The Kel Asouf, literally 'people who live all alone' or 'people who talk to no one', were mischievous spirits or demons who lived in dark and empty places such as caves, holes in the ground, trees and so forth, and were believed traditionally by Tuareg to cause all manner of misfortunes, accidents and illnesses, even to kill humans and animals by entering their bodies. Even more widespread was the belief in *tehot*, the 'evil eye' or 'evil mouth', to which I alluded earlier. Laudatory words expressing desire or envy, especially when applied to the animals, family or possessions of others, are sedulously avoided for fear of invoking *tehot*, the force of which is believed to harm men and even kill animals.

I watched Mokhtar carefully as he began to prepare tea and what I assumed to be *tagella*, the unleavened bread that Tuareg cook in the hot sand and ashes under the fire, and wondered. Was his veil below his mouth because of his status as an old man, or because in his rapidly modernising world he no longer believed in such things as the Kel Asouf and *tehot*, or simply because he was alone?

His two sons and the herdboy were in the *oued*, a couple of hundred metres beyond the camp, milking some of the goats before taking them out to graze for the day. I remembered the times of drought I had experienced in the 1960s when I was living in Dag

Rali camps in the high mountains of Atakor. There had been several years of insufficient rain, the grazing was impoverished, and herd sizes had been cut to a minimum. Fresh milk was scarce. Mokhtar's herd was large, numbering perhaps two hundred, and this probably accounted for the rudimentary nature of his camp – I guessed that it was just one of many that he occupied for a few days at a time as he kept the herd moving from one part of the valley to another in search of grazing. I wondered if Bouiya, with his one leg and his crutches, would go with the herd or stay in the camp.

I got up and dressed: trousers, boots, sweater and jacket. It was still cold. I felt a momentary regret that I could not shave or wash, then walked over to join Mokhtar. He gave me a friendly greeting, asked if I had slept well, and passed me a glass of tea, warm and sweet. In daylight he seemed smaller and frailer than he had the night before, but I suspected that like most Tuareg of his age he was well-accustomed to walking and riding long distances in arduous conditions. He made no attempt to adjust his veil, so that I could see almost all his face. Deep smile lines suggested a warmth of personality and a sense of humour that would make him a good travelling companion.

'This morning,' he said, as if reading my thoughts, 'I am going to look for camels.' I wanted to ask him how many he had; but to do so would be rude, for an older Tuareg like Mokhtar might consider it a temptation to *tehot*. Instead I asked him if they were nearby; I had seen no camels, tracks or droppings around the camp.

'They're around,' he said, waving an arm loosely towards the east but not taking his eyes from the teapots.

His enigmatic answer left me none the wiser as to the state or proximity of his camels. At that moment, Bahedi joined us and the subject of camels was ended for the time being. Bahedi was more smiles – to judge from what I could see of his face – than conversation at this time of the day. I wondered if he was naturally a slow riser, or whether he was simply enjoying the peace and solitude before returning to the bustle of Tamanrasset. Hosseyni, by contrast, was busily packing things back into the Land Cruiser, ready for their departure. We sat around the hearth for a while, eating a little *tagella* with our tea and watching as the boys prepared to take the goats out for the day in search of grazing. Bouiya went with them, deploying his one leg and crutches with the same speed and dexterity I had noticed the night before.

As the herd passed the Toyota Hosseyni signalled, first to the boys and then to Bahedi, who got up and went over to him. I watched uncertainly. When I saw Hosseyni slide beneath the Toyota's engine on his back, I realised it was probably a break-down. My own knowledge of car engines is as minimal as my mechanical skills, but Bahedi's calmness seemed to indicate that whatever wasn't working would soon be fixed. The boys hung around the vehicle, watching Hosseyni's contortions underneath it; the goats, well versed in their daily routine, carried on into the desert, oblivious of the pending crisis. Mokhtar and I remained by the hearth, each of us aware, I suspect, of our inability to do any-thing other than get in the way.

Bahedi soon returned. A ball-bearing in the starter motor was cracked, which meant that a push-start was the only way to get the engine going. Unfortunately, Hosseyni had parked in the lowest point of a slight depression. How could we possibly manage a push-start? Nevertheless, for nearly an hour we tried to defy Newton's law of gravity, exhausting ourselves in the process. All we managed to do was shift the Toyota about a hundred and fifty metres further away from the camp – and there we left it, marooned, forlorn, and looking more like a denizen of a second-hand-car lot than a new-fangled 'ship of the desert'. No one, however, least of all Bahedi, seemed unduly perturbed by this setback. His air was that of a man killing time until the breakdown truck arrived. With no more pushing to be done, the boys went off to catch up with the herd. Mokhtar, who had kept his own counsel throughout all the pushing and shoving, picked up a thin rope halter and sauntered off eastwards in search of his camels. Hosseyni, after a short discussion with Bahedi, set off alone on foot, hoping to find help in the little village of Mertoutek some twenty kilometres away.

By half-past ten the sun was high in the sky and the camp site was deserted apart from Bahedi, me, and the dead Toyota, half-hidden by a cluster of scrub tamarisk. Bahedi appeared to be quite unruffled by events, but it seemed undiplomatic, at such an early stage, to ask him how long he thought we might be stuck here, he waiting for Hosseyni to find a tow and I for Mokhtar and his camels. At least we had plenty of food and fresh water.

A hundred metres or so in front of Mokhtar's makeshift camp was a huge acacia, and with the heat of the day now upon us, Bahedi and I decided to set up a temporary hearth in its shade. The many acacias dotted across the plains immediately surrounding the Tefedest give the area a profoundly 'African' ambience. Slow-growing and very hard, acacia is much valued by Tuareg for its firewood. Bahedi reckoned this specimen must be at least a hundred years old.

We carried over the box of food supplies and cooking utensils, and laid out blankets on a patch of ground that we cleared of goat droppings and the vicious thorn-encrusted acacia twigs that carpeted the ground under the tree. This was my first full day in the open desert, and in the course of it memories, smells and sensations flooded back to me. Most of the memories were of days spent in the camps of Khabte and other Dag Rali, when the pace of life sometimes seemed interminably slow, time moving, quite literally, with the sun. The smells had begun to come back to me as soon as I entered Mokhtar's makeshift camp the night before. In camp the smell of goat – their live bodies, their roughly-tanned skins and their milk and soured butter – permeates everything. But here, away from the camp and the herd, I began to pick up the scents of some of the dozens of aromatic herbs that abound in Ahaggar, such as *tehergelé* and *tinhert*, which Tuareg love to add to their tea for their lemon and mint fragrances.

This morning, as soon as the sun had begun to warm things up, one of the more unpleasant and irritating memories of desert life also came back to me: the flies. They had not bothered me in Tamanrasset, probably because with rubbish everywhere they had more appetising matter on which to gorge themselves. Here in the open desert, they hounded with a vengeance. I don't know if the Saharan fly is generically much different from its relations in other parts of the world – I suspect not – but I would back it in any competition based on durability, perseverance, and the ability to drive one mad. The reason for their bountiful presence around the acacia was not far to seek. Mokhtar had evidently delved into the food supplies before the rest of us were up, found the meat Hosseyni had bought in the Tamanrasset market, cut it into portions and then skewered them out in the thorny lower branches of the acacia, presumably to mature and tenderise. I looked askance at my food supply for the next week or two, a seething mass of flies, all desperate to lay their eggs in perpetuation of one of nature's more unpleasant reproductive cycles.

We made a new fire and, travellers being exempt from a rigorous observance of the Ramadan fast, spent the next hour or so preparing lunch: lentils with onions, potatoes, carrots, a few chillies, and some pieces of mutton which I was relieved to see came from the food container and not the tree. Bahedi did most of the work, and as he worked we talked, among other things about how flies see. I demonstrated how the fact that they are able to perceive lateral but not vertical movement could be used to accelerate their execution. I think he was impressed by the success rate of my steady hand, lowered almost to within touching distance before swatting. It was a trivial yet satisfying pursuit, and helped to idle away the time.

After lunch we attempted to sleep, but the flies gave us no respite. Instead, we began at last to consider who might return first, Mokhtar or Hosseyni. Bahedi thought Mokhtar would spend all day searching for and then rounding up his camels, but if Hosseyni managed to find someone in Mertoutek with a suitable vehicle, he should be back fairly soon. But it was Mokhtar who returned first, and without any camels. He came loping over the low col that marked the watershed between the *Oued* Mertoutek and the *Oued* Irharhar to the east of us, swinging the thin halter rope in time with his step and seemingly in good spirits. He stopped for no more than a few minutes, long enough to explain that his camels must be in the other direction and drink some water, before setting off up the tamarisk-shrouded bed of the *Oued* Mertoutek to the north-west. It struck me as strange that a Tuareg should not know the whereabouts of his camels; but I was aware that they are apt to roam far and wide if left unhobbled, and thought he probably knew their inclinations.

By four in the afternoon there was still no sound of an engine heralding Hosseyni's return, and I was beginning to wonder if his search, like Mokhtar's, was proving fruitless. I also wanted to explore my surroundings, so I set off to climb the granite ridge to the east of our camp. It was a trek of a kilometre or so and an ascent not far short of three hundred metres. I anticipated that the view from the summit would be worth the effort.

As is so often the case in the desert, I found that what had looked like a summit from our camp site was in reality a false one. On breasting it, I found there was still another small valley to negotiate, and another climb of about a hundred metres on the other side. So on I went, over bare rock so old (some six hundred million years) and so long exposed to weathering that whole chunks of it crumbled under even a modest kick from my boots.

When I finally reached the true summit, the view was as breathtaking as I had hoped. The horizon stretched away for perhaps two hundred kilometres in a great arc from the north through to the south-east, and I gazed out across this extraordinary land with its distant, pale mauve mountain ranges, the barren plains between, and the valleys dotted with acacia and tamarisk trees, their meandering lines of scrubby, dried-up pasture seeming to feel their way warily out from the feet of the mountains into the open desert beyond. Here and there the sun picked up patches of bright-yellow sand that had been blown up against the mountains and rocky outcrops, sometimes forming into sweeps of dunes. But in this part of the Sahara there is more mountain, rock and gravel than sand. The vast expanse of rugged and almost primeval emptiness opening out before me brought no feelings of fear, rather the warmth of familiarity, such as the Kel Ahaggar themselves must experience even more intensely, for this land is their home. Like them, I found a feeling of reassurance in being able to recognise and identify almost every feature of the landscape before me.

In the middle distance the mountain range of Tourha (from which Mokhtar's section of the Ait Lowayen took its name, Kel Tourha) stood out like a line of silver sails as the setting sun reflected off its smooth, grey granite slopes. Beyond Tourha I could see the peaks of Serkout and the Djebel Telertheba, both rising to more than two thousand metres. In the old days, Telertheba was an important landmark for the caravans that carried salt from the nearby deposits in the plain of Amadror to Niger to exchange for millet. In the furthest distance, about two hundred and fifty kilometres away, I could just make out the dim line of the great Tassili escarpment that runs like a huge protective battlement around much of Ahaggar.

But it was the foreground, between me and the shining silver-grey flanks of Tourha, which most attracted my attention: this was the great valley of Irharhar, the largest *oued* leading out of Ahaggar. In prehistoric times it is possible that water flowed regularly through the valley; elephants, giraffes and other wild animals certainly browsed and watered here. Now it was dry, except perhaps for a day or two once every few years following heavy rains in Ahaggar. Its flat valley two or three kilometres wide was full of acacia trees, stunted thorn bushes and scrubby, dried-up pasture. You could easily ride across it without getting much more than a hint that you were crossing one of the longest valleys in Africa.

Somewhere in the vicinity, possibly not far from here, lay the site of one of France's most gruesome setbacks, the story and memory of which is seared into French colonial history.

It was proposed to reconnoitre a route through Ahaggar for a trans-Saharan railway to connect France's North African territories with her sub-Saharan and Central African possessions. The fact that the Americans had succeeded in building a railway across their continent eleven years previously gave further impetus to the hare-brained scheme. One of the main reasons for choosing the Ahaggar route was the supposed friendliness of the Tuareg: the minister responsible ignored the advice of his own Bureau des Affaires Indigènes, who pointed out that Tuareg preferred to raid rather than trade for their needs.

The ill-fated expedition that left Laghouat, in the north Algerian Sahara, in November 1880 under the command of Colonel Flatters consisted of ninety-two men: ten French army officers and engineers, forty-seven Arab soldiers of the Algerian *Tirailleurs* with two French NCOs and two orderlies, and thirty-one Chaamba guides and cameleers. Somewhere close to where I was now sitting, the Tuareg had lured them into a trap and killed more than fifty of them. Of the forty left alive, only twelve survived the terrible three-month trek back to the town of Ouargla in the northern Sahara. The story of the massacre and the ghastly ordeal of its survivors so horrified the government that the gory details were kept from the French public, and further colonial expansion into the Sahara was halted for almost twenty years.

I stayed there until dusk, watching the light leaching out of the great valley of Irharhar as the sun fell away behind me, and as I watched I wondered just how far away from this spot the massacre of Flatters and his companions had taken place. It was a chilling thought. It was twilight by the time I started my descent, and I had to pick my way carefully. Already, I realised, I had abandoned the minute enumerations of European time and was beginning to think like a Tuareg again, my day more sparingly divided into the periods relating to dawn, midday, afternoon and night. Such a simplification immediately reduces life to a much more dignified and humane pace.

When I came in sight of the camp again I could see figures moving around the fire. The goat herd and the boys had returned, as had Mokhtar and Hosseyni. But there was no sign of camels, or of a rescue vehicle.

Conversation in the camp was muted. Hosseyni was particularly subdued, and I deemed it wiser to wait for Bahedi to tell me what was going on. Mokhtar's story was simple: he had not found any camels, and would look again in the morning. Hosseyni's news was not quite as bad as I had feared it might be: he had found someone in Mertoutek with a Land Rover, but to return at once with him would have been to miss the evening meal of Ramadan, and they would therefore come to us tomorrow. Hosseyni had returned to tell us this, and after he had eaten would set off again on foot to Mertoutek, so that he could direct the Land Rover to us in the morning.

'You must be exhausted,' I commiserated. 'You had to walk the whole way?'

'It will be sixty kilometres when I get back there tonight,' he grumbled, his tone more sullen than weary. I had not failed to appreciate that it was entirely because of me that we had come to this remote corner of Ahagger; although it was not my fault that the starter-motor had broken or that Hosseyni had parked at the bottom of a slope, I felt sure the slight air of strain hanging over the camp was at least in part attributable to my presence.

Hosseyni did not linger once he had eaten. An hour or so after he had left, with just Mokhtar, Bahedi and myself drinking tea around the fire, the atmosphere seemed a little more relaxed, and I felt able to mention camels again, wondering what I would do if tomorrow's search proved as fruitless as today's.

'Ah,' exclaimed Mokhtar, apparently in good spirits, 'it is my eyes that are the problem. I can't see the camels. When you come back, you must bring me some binoculars. Then I will find them easily.'

'Is his eyesight really that bad?' I asked Bahedi when Mokhtar left the hearth for a few minutes.

'I don't know, but he always brings up the subject of binoculars.'

'Does he actually have any camels?' It seemed an appropriate time to confess the doubts that had been growing upon me since Mokhtar's first empty-handed return to the camp.

'He says he does. A disease killed off a lot of camels in this area last year, so maybe he has a problem. But if he hasn't any of his own any more, he'll find someone else who has.'

'Wouldn't it be easier for all concerned if I returned to Tamanrasset tomorrow with you and Hosseyni?'

'Oh, no. Mokhtar will find camels. And if he doesn't, Hosseyni says that Sid Ahmed, who is coming tomorrow, will make his Land Rover available, as long as I can provide him with enough fuel.'

This comment eased my mind a little, and I thought to ask why Hosseyni had seemed so down in the dumps.

'Two vehicles passed him this morning and didn't even stop. That didn't make his day!'

'But everyone stops in the desert!' My tone of surprise was in truth a little forced, because I had a feeling I could guess what the vehicles were doing and why they hadn't stopped. So, I suspected, could Bahedi. What came to mind was all those tracks we had seen yesterday, which Bahedi had so airily suggested were probably made by *contrabandiers*. Surely the vehicles that had passed Hosseyni must also have been *contrabandiers*. Why else had they not stopped?

Bahedi had shrugged slightly at my last remark. 'Yes, normally.'

There was something I had been wanting to bring up with Bahedi since our first meeting, but had refrained from doing so for fear that it was too politically sensitive. This was my opportunity. 'Could it be Hadj Bettu's people?' I asked, as matter-of-factly as possible.

Bahedi turned and looked at me in surprise: 'You know Hadj Bettu?'

I told him what little I knew. From what I had been able to learn in London it appeared that Hadj Bettu had established himself in the early 1990s as something of a local 'warlord' in Algeria's southern Sahara, stock-piling arms and heaven knows what else in and around Tamanrasset and running his own private army south of the border in Niger. There were rumours of his involvement in the assassination of Algeria's president, Mohammed Boudiaf, in 1992. The government had claimed that Islamic fundamentalists were responsible, but many analysts specialising in Algerian affairs consider that the deed was organised by the army-led 'political-financial mafia', and that Hadj Bettu may also have been implicated, since Boudiaf had recently ordered a crack-down on corruption and was well aware of Hadj Bettu's desert fiefdom.

Whether or not Bettu was indeed involved in the assassination, the rumours certainly seemed to have made the military-backed government sit up and think about what might be going on in this remote desert region. They moved quickly, changing the political map of Algeria by turning Ahaggar into the country's sixth military region and thus bringing it under the direct control of the military high command in Algiers. The country had enough problems to contend with in the north; the last thing the government wanted was a crisis in the south as well, especially when Algeria was so dependent economically on its Saharan oil and gas deposits.

'It's not Bettu,' said Bahedi. 'He's been in gaol since about 'ninety-two.'

This made me feel rather stupid, and I began to realise just how out of touch I was. Bahedi then amused me with the information that there is now an expression current in the north of Algeria describing someone who suddenly makes a lot of money as a Hadj Bettu.

'Most people here reckon he made a lot of money out of smuggling,' said Bahedi, 'but I think he was quite liked and even respected, especially by the poor. He helped them a lot.'

If those tracks and those passing vehicles weren't to be laid at Hadj Bettu's door, had someone stepped into his shoes? The thought was a little scary. Modern brigandage was like a hydra with many heads: had another 'head' taken over from Hadj Bettu in this part of the Sahara?

That night I slept for the first time in my small, one-man tent. As I lay in it, wondering what the morrow might bring in the way of transport or how much longer I might have to remain here, broken down and with no camels, I began to get a sense that the open spaces of the Sahara, once the domain of nomads, had been taken over by more shadowy and dangerous elements. It was not a subject on which any of my travelling companions seemed at all keen to proffer an opinion.

As I had suspected would be the case, Mokhtar did not spend much time looking for camels in the morning. He was back in the camp even before the goats had been taken out for the day, muttering about it being easier to look for camels with a vehicle.

This, when it finally arrived at about ten in the morning, turned out to have a 'face' like Thomas the Tank Engine and its rattletrap condition reminded me of those ingenious toys African children make from wire coat hangers and other assorted pieces of scrap. It was a squat little Land Rover, cab in front and pick-up behind, and I later learnt it was upwards of twenty-five years old. Closer inspection revealed that it could have been an escapee from the out-patients' department of a car repair hospital, so much of it was held together with pieces of cloth and other odd materials – albeit clearly applied with a great deal of tender loving care. Its owner, Sid Ahmed, dressed in clean white *gandoura*, white *chech* and veil, filled the space behind the steering wheel. As he descended to greet us the vehicle rose on its springs, breathing what I swear was a sigh of relief. He was a huge man and, as I was to discover, immensely strong.

Greeting me briefly but courteously, Sid Ahmed went into a huddle, first with Hosseyni about tow-starting the Toyota, then with Bahedi about my travel arrangements – and Mokhtar's. After half an hour, all was agreed. The food supplies and sufficient fuel were to be transferred to Sid Ahmed's Land Rover, which he would rent to me, with himself as driver, until Mokhtar could find his camels; failing that, we would rendezvous the following week with Bahedi and Hosseyni. To save Mokhtar the indignity of losing his income as a cameleer, it was agreed that he would be paid at a cameleer's rate to act as cook and 'special' guide – not, I felt sure, that there was the least uncertainty about where we might be going, for I was convinced Mokhtar had had his social tour planned from the moment I explained my interest in the local nomadic camps.

Within a matter of minutes Mokhtar's temporary camp, and my home for two nights, was abandoned to the desert: only the surrounding branches and sticks of the shelter, the carpet of goat droppings and our tracks remained. The Toyota tow-started without fuss and bore Bahedi and Hosseyni off to Tamanrasset, and the boys set out with the goat herd to wend their way up the *oued* to Mokhtar's main camp. Mokhtar and I climbed into Sid Ahmed's Land Rover, Mokhtar squashed into the middle over the gear lever while I bunched myself up against the passenger door, which looked and felt as if it might fly open at any moment. But I was glad to be on the way again as we turned out of the camp area and headed northwards up the tamarisk-shrouded *Oued* Mertoutek on our great adventure into the next millennium – for it was already 30 December 1999.

We followed the *oued* for six or eight kilometres before branching out on to a plain not much more than a kilometre wide, bounded by the mountains of Tefedest on the left and the ridge I had climbed the previous evening on our right. The surface of the plain was gravel, with here and there a thin coating of sand, easier to drive on than the heavy sand of the *oued*. Vegetation was patchy. The acacia trees thinned out quite quickly away from where the mountains joined the plain, giving way to more isolated, stunted thorn bushes and, in the shallow depressions and dried-up rivulets, scanty tufts of scrubby, desiccated pasture waiting with eternal patience for the rare down-pour of rain that would herald regeneration.

We hadn't gone far before we found our first camel, its pile of bleached bones surpassing any toothpaste advertisement for white-ness. 'Drought?' I asked, addressing my question specifically to Sid Ahmed and knowing the answer.

'No. Probably the disease that killed most of the camels around here last year.'

I then asked Mokhtar what type of disease it had been, and whether anything had been done to overcome it. But he didn't seem to know, and I got the impression that it been localised within this area. I hadn't suspected him of lying about his camels, but I had sus-pected the previous day's searches to be a charade prompted by the need to save face in front of the men from Tamanrasset. For a Tuareg nomad not to have camels was humiliating, particularly when Bahedi was a potential source of tourist income – should tourists ever return. 'How many did you lose?' I asked him.

'About twenty,' he replied. Twenty camels was probably an exag-geration of his personal wealth, but seemed about right for his family group as a whole.

The Land Rover putt-putt-putted slowly northwards, rarely exceeding twenty-five kilometres an hour as Sid Ahmed nursed it along the dusty plain beside the *Oued* Mertoutek. About an hour later we came across our second camel – three of them, indeed, being led northwards by a Tuareg on foot. We slowly overhauled him and stopped to talk. He was a Kel Rezzi, dressed in a traditional indigo-blue *gandoura* and veil, slight of build and travelling from Tamanrasset to Illizi, some fifteen days further to the north-east. The camels, he told us, had been brought up from the plains of Tamesna in northern Niger, the traditional camel-grazing grounds for the Kel Ahaggar, and he had bought them in Tamanrasset. Two of the animals appeared to be well-bred and in fine condition. As he soon explained, the bigger of the two, a superb beast that carried no baggage, was for the camel races at Illizi.

'What are these camel races?' I asked Sid Ahmed.

'They hold big races at Illizi, now. It's an annual event and people come from all over. You can get rich: a good camel can make a lot of money.'

'Who races?'

'Anyone, especially Tuareg and the old enemy – Chaamba. Tuareg love to race against Chaamba and beat them.'

As we watched them striding off on their long journey, I thought it would have been fun to place an each-way bet on that camel, assuming that some sort of betting went on.

Along this eastern side of the Tefedest the landscape was almost constantly changing. The plain on which we were driving was about twelve hundred metres above sea level. On our left the bulbous silver–grey granite of the Tefedest massif ballooned up steeply into a line of central peaks at around two and a half thousand metres. One of the peaks was almost a perfect dome, slowly weathered to this shape by millions of years of erosion. Every few kilometres a valley emptied from the mountains and cut across the plain, making for the great valley of Irharhar four or five kilometres to our right. Some of these smaller valleys were quite thick with tamarisk trees, which quickly gave away to acacias and stunted thorn bushes further 'downstream' as the valleys flowed out across the plain. You could tell how far away from the mountain you were by the texture and composition of the floors of these *oueds*. Nearer to the Tefedest they were coarse gravel mixed with stones and boulders washed out of the mountains in the occasional but violent floods. Further downstream, towards the Irharhar, the beds became sandier. To our right, the ridge that I had climbed and that we had been following broke up gradually into a succession of rocky outcrops and finally disappeared altogether, leaving nothing but gently sloping plain between us and the Irharhar valley. Where we stopped to speak to the Kel Rezzi camel racer the plain was a perfectly flat gravel carpet with a suggestion of pink and red in it, but completely devoid of vegetation. The rest of the plain was more undulating, dissected by the multitude of *oueds* crossing it and studded with piles of boulders and more solid-looking rock outcrops.

At around midday we stopped in the shade of an acacia for what was to become the daily ritual of lunch. Sid Ahmed, who was observing the fast, would immediately stretch out on the ground and cover himself in a blanket to sleep out the two or three hours. Mokhtar, taking his role as cook very seriously, would ask me what I fancied. Having little appetite, I would suggest that I leave the choice to him. And so it was. Each day while Sid Ahmed, Mokhtar and I were travelling together, Mokhtar provided me with four-star service, working his way through the abundant supplies Bahedi had left with us: plenty of flour for *tagella*, various pastas, rice, cooking oil, plenty of fresh potatoes, onions, carrots and tomatoes, tinned lentils and beans, various tinned spices, a couple of tins of olives (which I greatly appreciated), fresh oranges – and, of course, Mokhtar's delectable fly blown meat. I pretended I was not a great meat-eater, which pleased him enormously. As I watched him tucking into three good meals a day (he also ate breakfast) and recalled the absence of food I had noted at his makeshift camp, I wondered whether he had been observing Ramadan prior to our arrival.

'Is everyone now keeping *karem* [the fast]?' I asked him, knowing that in the past many Tuareg, being fairly lax Moslems, found reasons to avoid it.

'Oh, yes,' he answered. 'Take Mertoutek: three years ago, hardly anyone kept *karem*; now everyone does.' I had noticed in Tamanrasset how much more widely used Arabic was now than formerly, and had heard from both Bahedi and Claudia how much stronger Islam had become in the region since I was last here.

'What about you, then?' I asked, expecting him to refer to the exemption for travellers.

'It's the doctor. He told me that *karem* wouldn't do my eyes any good.' Those whose health is poor are also exempt from the fast, but I wondered whether it was the doctor who first raised the subject of *karem*, or Mokhtar. I couldn't imagine a doctor telling a patient to be sure to eat well for the good of his *eyes*. Or could I? No wonder these nomads were such survivors, I thought: they had native cunning in abundance, and an answer for everything, even ideology. I didn't ask him which doctor's surgery he'd attended, though I knew from Bahedi that he had accompanied his wife to Tamanrasset four years before, when she was ill with heart trouble. They had actually flown her, on her own, to a hospital in Algiers for treatment, an experience which had terrified her.

Now that we were on to medical matters, I thought I might raise the question of Bouiya's leg. 'He lost it four years ago, when he was fourteen,' Mokhtar told me.

'How did it happen?'

'He was at the *internat* [boarding school] at Ideles. His leg swelled up and they took him to the hospital in Tamanrasset where they said it should be cut off.'

It was plain that neither he nor Bouiya himself had any clear idea of the medical background. The leg, he kept repeating to me, was *gonflé* (swollen). And that was that. He spoke of it quite unquestioningly, without any hint of criticism of Bouiya's medical treatment – or, perhaps, the lack of it. It wasn't easy to guess what might have happened. One could envisage an infection getting into the foot and being left untreated until it became so serious through lack of medical attention and drugs that amputation was the only option. There were also any number of poisonous or otherwise highly dangerous plants in the region that might have pricked or cut his foot, not to mention snakebite – any one of these might have made amputation the only way to save his life. Whatever had happened, Mokhtar had accepted it with equanimity.

'And Mohammed?' I asked, referring to his eldest son. 'He's doing his national service now?'

Mokhtar chuckled. 'Oh, no – he's got an exemption.'

'What do you mean?' Did Mohammed also have a medical affliction?

'I went and saw the army and told them that with Bouiya's one leg and my eyes, I needed Mohammed here to look after the camels.' This time, he spoke as if the loss of Bouiya's leg was tantamount to a payment or sacrifice already made to the state.

'So why', I asked drily, 'hasn't Mohammed been rounding up more camels?'

'Because he's been working in an office in Illizi,' he said, breaking into a cackle of laughter. Algeria's generals may have much to answer for, but in their dealings with Tuareg such as Mokhtar they are perhaps entitled to a certain sympathy.

We had not driven far after our lunch-time siesta when we came across an unearthly scene. Hundreds of dead, almost petrified, ashen-coloured tree-trunks, branches and other debris lay strewn across a shallow, sandy-bottomed basin about a kilometre wide and perhaps twice as long. There was not a vestige of any living matter.

'What on earth is this?' I asked.

'The remains of a huge flood,' Sid Ahmed replied. 'In 1954.'

'Are you sure it was 1954?'

'Well, it was a few years before I was born, so I can't be sure, but it was about then. Maybe a year or two one way or the other.' I asked him to stop the Land Rover for a minute so that I could dig a rather battered book out of my rucksack. I had brought Louis Carl and Joseph Petit's *Tefedest: A Journey to the Heart of the Sahara* with me for a particular reason: exactly fifty years ago this very week they had led the first expedition into Tefedest to search for and record prehistoric cave paintings. Indeed, my trip to the Tefedest had been partly planned in the knowledge that it would coincide with this fiftieth anniversary. The expedition was made in 1949–50 but the book was only published in 1954, and a note had been added regarding the rains during that interim period. I soon found the reference: after five years without a drop, there had been exceptional rainfall in the winters of 1949–50, 1950–51 and 1951–52. Travellers recorded the extraordinary sight of mountains covered in chest-high vegetation. Desert marches became long strolls in oceans of sweet-smelling flowers which left generous deposits of pollen on the clothes of men and the coats of camels. During this time, thousands of head of camels which had taken refuge in the pastures of Tamesna in Niger returned to Ahaggar.

'I can remember well,' chipped in Mokhtar, who would have been a young boy at the time. 'There were torrential rains and floods. Everything here – trees, plants, animals – just got ripped out of the ground and washed down the *oued*.' And here we were, in another period of aridity, and here were those same remains which had been washed out of the mountains by the floodwaters almost fifty years ago.

It reminded me of photographs of the woods and forests outside Hiroshima after the blast, and my first thought had been that it must have had something to do with the old nuclear test site at In Eker, only about eighty kilometres to the west.

'Do you remember In Eker?' I asked, addressing myself deliberately to Sid Ahmed rather than Mokhtar. As the older man, Mokhtar's memories were probably more accurate and pertinent, and I therefore wanted him to recall them in his own time, and not in response to such direct questioning.

'I worked there, you know.'

'At In Eker? But weren't you too young?' The base must surely have been closed by the time Sid Ahmed was old enough to go out to work.

'I worked at the mountain next to In Eker,' he said. I wasn't sure what he meant by this, but before I could follow it up Mokhtar, as I had hoped, was ready to add his piece.

'I remember the lorries and the helicopter,' he said.

'What lorries and helicopter?'

'After the "bang", three lorries and a helicopter came to check on fumes.'

'What fumes?' I asked.

'I don't know,' said Mokhtar. 'That's just what the French said: that they wanted to check on *les vapeurs*.'

'Where did the lorries go, and what did the people who came in them say?'

'They came to Mertoutek – nowhere else, as far as I know. They didn't say anything very much, just that they were checking on *les vapeurs* and that there was nothing to worry about.'

'Did they say anything about an accident, or give you any warnings about possible danger?'

'No, nothing at all.'

'Except that a lot of people died,' interjected Sid Ahmed.

I had always suspected that people had died after the test, but this was the first time I had ever heard anyone actually say so. 'How many died?'

'Ten or twelve,' said Sid Ahmed.

Mokhtar had been counting up names on his fingers. 'I think it may have been about fifteen,' he said. 'Seven died in one night. I can't remember the others exactly.'

'What do you mean? That you can't remember *who* died, or *when* they died?'

'When they died. But it was all at about the same time.'

'What did they die of?' I asked, though I doubted that Mokhtar had any knowledge of radiation sickness or its symptoms.

'*La grippe*,' he said, as if that explained everything. Yes, I thought. How many deaths in French colonial territories have been written off as *la grippe* (influenza)? And Mokhtar's tally didn't include the children I knew had died in the Tamanrasset hospital some years later.

'And that wasn't all,' said Sid Ahmed. 'Several people were born later with deformed limbs – arms and legs. Also, many animals died – slowly.'

'Are there still people alive with such deformities?' Concrete proof might be needed if anything as unlikely as an investigation were ever to be held.

'Oh yes, I can introduce you to some.'

'And there were many plants', Mokhtar chipped in, 'which just died out in the area. It's only been in the last few years that they have come back again.'

We drove on slowly up the eastern side of Tefedest, towards the well at Adjelil. There were a number of encampments there, at which we were going to stay. What little conversation passed between us consisted mostly of answering Sid Ahmed's questions about where and how I had travelled in Ahaggar when I was first here. The subject of In Eker seemed to have put a bit of a dampener on the afternoon. Mokhtar and Sid Ahmed had confirmed what I had long suspected: no one had ever come to tell the two hundred or so people of Mertoutek what had happened at In Eker, and what effect it might have had on them. No medical assistance was ever afforded to the villagers of Mertoutek and the surrounding nomads; and if the French military had ever undertaken any survey of or research in the region to assess the extent of radioactive contamination, it had certainly been kept very secret.

A crime had been committed against the people of this region, and it had been covered up. France had entered Ahaggar in 1880 in a disastrous bout of absurd colonial bombast, wanting to build a railway across the Sahara. She had departed a little more than three generations later following a similar burst of bombastic nationalism, trying to match the USA and UK as a nuclear power. Both events had been surrounded by mistakes, and on both occasions the French government had tried to hide the truth. The only difference, as far as I could see, was that the first time round it was French soldiers and auxiliaries who paid the price for these mistakes, whereas in 1961 it was innocent people, the inhabitants of Mertoutek and the surrounding Tefedest, who had suffered and died.

5

The mothers' brothers of Adjelil

B Y THE TIME we reached the *oued* at Adjelil the sun had fallen behind the peaks of the Tefedest and we were in their shadow. Adjelil was a big valley, full of tamarisk trees, and we drove up its sandy bed for about a kilometre before we came to the well. Sid Ahmed told me it had been rebuilt by the *commune* in 1995, which explained why it now took the form of a large concrete culvert pipe sticking up about two feet out of the ground, with two tree-trunks on either side to support a metal bar and pulley-wheel. We stopped at the well to top up the jerricans with water. Sid Ahmed checked the radiator and tinkered with the engine, and then we carried on up the *oued* towards the two encampments which were our goal.

The first, a few hundred metres further up the *oued*, comprised two tents. One was a large military-looking affair, the like of which I had never seen before in a Tuareg camp; the other was an older, more traditionally makeshift arrangement consisting of a mixture of skins and tarpaulin draped over wooden tent poles interspersed with tree branches. The second encampment, which I could just see in the distance, was about a kilometre further on up the *oued*.

Both camps were pitched on high ground on the bank of the *oued*, to be safe from any sudden flood. It is on the face of it a curious fact that a not inconsiderable number of Tuareg have drowned in Ahaggar over the years. Rain, sometimes heavy, can fall at almost any time of the year in Ahaggar, but especially at the end of summer and in winter. And when it rains, the speed of the run-off in the steep

73

mountain valleys is such that they can become raging torrents within minutes. Earlier that afternoon we had seen the sort of thing the floods of the early 1950s had done.

From the outset I had thought that the occupants of these camps must be related in some way or another to Mokhtar, but assumed it to be only distantly, as members of the same descent group, the Ait Lowayen Kel Tourha. What I did not discover until we were actually approaching the first camp was that it belonged to Sid Ahmed's sister and her husband – a complete surprise, for I had had no idea that Sid Ahmed had nomadic kinsmen; the second camp, it turned out, belonged to Mokhtar's sister and *her* husband.

This was immensely exciting, for it meant that each man was visiting as the mother's brother of the children living in the respective camps. In traditional Tuareg society, at least until the end of French colonial rule, the mother's brother, or *anet ma* as he is known in Tamahak, was an immensely significant figure. Indeed, for a number of very complex 'anthropological' reasons this was the pivotal relationship in traditional Tuareg society, and around it centred many important political, economic and social rights and obligations.

In the first camp, Sid Ahmed's sister Fatimata – Fata – lived in the big tent with her three young children. The tent was a 'present' (I later learned that all Tuareg nomads had been given one) from the government. Fata was probably in her late twenties or early thirties, and though she had some of her brother's height, which gave her a certain elegance, she did not share his girth. When we arrived, her black headcloth was draped over most of her face, as was becoming in the presence of men and strangers. But as the evening wore on she let it fall, and I could see that she had a lively and intelligent face with an attractive smile and deep brown eyes. She was clearly very close to her brother, talking to him intimately and leaning against him as we sat on carpets around the hearth outside the tent. Her laughter was most engaging. Her husband was away at Ideles, one of the largest villages outside Tamanrasset, about a hundred and eighty kilometres to the south-east. I gathered he had some sort of job there, but Sid Ahmed could not elaborate as his sister was still vague about the details. The older and tattier tent was occupied by a younger girl and two children, who remained in the background and to whom I was not introduced. Sid Ahmed described her merely as a 'cousin'.

After the conventional courtesies of greeting had been gone through and we were sitting around the hearth drinking tea, I raised the subject of the mother's brother, asking whether both Mokhtar and Sid Ahmed were not *anet ma* to all the various children in the camps. 'Ah!' cackled Mokhtar in his high-pitched voice, 'he knows the mother's brother!'

'What do you know of the *anet ma*?' asked Sid Ahmed, clearly delighted at having his special role brought to public attention.

'Well,' I said, 'isn't the *anet ma* meant to bring lots of affection and presents?' Like a fairy godfather, I thought.

'Presents!' cried Mokhtar, almost beside himself with laughter at the idea being a source of such *largesse*. '*Tidet, tidet houllan!* (That's the truth!) – *Issan tamahak!* (He knows Tamahak!)'

The mother's brother was important because of the predominantly matrilineal basis on which Tuareg society was traditionally organised: a child always belonged to the same descent group as his mother's brother, at whose death he traditionally received certain symbols of his uncle's power, such as his sword, his finest robes and his religious amulets.

Traditionally, too, another importance of the mother's brother was as a continual source of income, not only by way of the gifts he might give, but because a nephew had the right to ask his maternal uncle for virtually anything he needed. The uncle could not legitimately refuse such requests, and should he do so, the nephew had the right to take whatever it was he needed.

Some of the earliest European travellers among the Tuareg, noting this custom but misinterpreting it, saw it as a form of institutionalised thieving and were accordingly disapproving of Tuareg morality. Correctly understood, however, it explains the survival of this ancient pastoral society for so long in such a miserly environment, one in which natural hazards like drought and disease, not to mention human pillagers, have with alarming regularity threatened to wipe out the productive resources of individual groups and families. The key lies in the extension of the idea of the *anet ma* to include many other maternal kinsmen, who because of the custom for a married couple to settle in the husband's community tended to live in other social groups and encampments, often far away. A nephew therefore had many such beneficial 'uncles', usually living in far-off places, to whom he could turn in the event of disaster, exercising his right to claim anything he might need. Far from being 'institutionalised thieving', this very special relationship, embedded in the complex fabric of kinship and custom, gave the Tuareg a form of insurance, almost like a credit network: in times of disaster livestock could if necessary be shared over a broad social and geographical base.

I was now able to observe the modern expression of this relationship, quite apart from the affection Sid Ahmed was lavishing on his sister's children. The 'presents' today took the form of the abundant food supplies in the back of the Land Rover, and that vehicle's availability for any necessary chores. On this occasion, it transpired that Fata and her 'cousin' wanted to check on what had been left at an abandoned settlement and garden some twenty kilometres further up the *oued*, in the very heart of the Tefedest mountains. The place was called Adjelil Tarhaouhaout, and the garden had been abandoned about fifteen years ago, so Mokhtar told me, when the Tuareg who worked it had moved to the village of Mertoutek. When there was good pasture in the area, the women from the camp would take the goats up the *oued* and stay in the old disused *zeribas* (reed huts) by the garden. There was also a venerable fig tree in the garden and a special type of melon which, from what Mokhtar told me, had continued to seed itself over the years.

Everyone was so relaxed and happy the following morning that it was ten o'clock before we finally set off for Adjelil Tarhaouhaout. Sid Ahmed was engrossed with his young nephews and niece, and Mokhtar walked up to his sister's camp to let her know that we would be camping with her for the next night or two. It took us almost two hours to cover the twenty kilometres to Adjelil Tarhaouhaout, Sid Ahmed inching the Land Rover over steep, boulder-strewn terrain at walking pace. The abandoned garden lay about a kilometre upstream from a series of *gueltas* or pools where a band of impermeable granite had had the effect of damming the *oued*, holding up its water-table. Fresh running water trickled over the smooth granite for some fifty metres, forming a series of clear rock pools surrounded by emerald green water grasses and sedges. Immediately above the *gueltas* a thick bed of fresh green reeds filled the valley and provided a herd of wild donkeys with abundant grazing. On the bank of the *oued*, stones marked the outline of a mosque presumably used by the Tuareg who once lived here.

From where we had stopped the Land Rover in the sandy bed of the *oued* just above the reed bed, I could see the remains of four reed huts about four hundred metres further up the valley. From this distance the former garden was barely visible, water and wind having long since obliterated all but its vaguest outline.

As soon as we arrived Fata and her cousin ran on up the valley to check on the two still-habitable huts they used when, occasionally, they brought the goats here. Sid Ahmed went to the *guelta*, glad of the chance to wash his white *chech* in clean running water, then covered himself with a blanket and retired for his siesta on the sand beside the Land Rover. Mokhtar suggested we should leave the women up at the huts, doing whatever it was they had come to do, and explore up there ourselves after we had eaten. As he began to prepare lunch for the pair of us, I decided to investigate our immediate surroundings, and set off to climb the steep, boulder-strewn valley-side in front of us. The view down the valley from this ridge was almost as magnificent as the one I had enjoyed above Mokhtar's camp two days earlier. Here I was at about two thousand metres, perhaps six hundred metres above the well at Adjelil but at least three hundred below the top peaks of the Tefedest. The V-shaped valley walls gave me a peep-show view across the Irharhar valley to the mountains of Tourha in the distance.

After lunch Mokhtar and I walked up to the reed huts and the garden, leaving Sid Ahmed under his blanket beside the vehicle. The women were busy in one of the huts and we explored the others, and the traces of the old garden. Two of the huts had long since been blown down, all that remained of them a few branches of old reed scattered over the ground, a broken enamel bowl, stone hearths and a few bits of old rope and matting, all testaments to their previous habitation. I calculated that with the four huts, possibly more, and perhaps two or three tents, as many as two dozen people might have formed a little community here. There was good fresh water, sufficient grazing, and the produce from the gardens. But, like so many other semi-nomadic Tuareg, these people had joined the exodus to the villages. The old fig tree looked rather forlorn, as did the self-seeded melons, which had only survived because they were growing beneath the protective skirts of a straggly thorn bush that kept animals from them. Mokhtar and I picked eight fruits – rather undersized treasure-trove – before calling to the women to let them know we were heading back to the Land Rover.

Before we left the *oued*, Mokhtar busied himself with burning a clump of dead grass, of a species I did not know, and then crushing the ashes into fine black powder. When it was the texture of graphite, he tipped it carefully into a tiny plastic pot which he then tied into the end of his *chech* for safekeeping. When I enquired what he was doing, he simply told me it was a medicine. 'For Nama,' he said.

I met Nama later that evening. Mokhtar's sister lived with her husband Kaouadis (pronounced 'Cowardice') and four children – two boys and two girls – at the higher of the two camps at Adjelil. Mokhtar and I moved our things to her camp, while Sid Ahmed remained with his sister. Kaouadis, at sixty-three or thereabouts, was five years older than Mokhtar and his first cousin, being the son of Mokhtar's father's brother.

Kaouadis, thin and two or three inches taller than Mokhtar, walked with the beginnings of a stoop. His eyes above his veil showed the same alert sparkle and hawkishness I had seen in those of so many Tuareg. Nama, a frail, slightly-built woman, was not well, I suspected. From the ages of her children and what Mokhtar had told me about her, she was probably nearer to forty than fifty, but looked much older. From the shape of her small, thin wrists and hands and the way she moved, I wondered if she was suffering the beginnings of arthritis or some sort of rheumatic complaint; I thought, too, of Mokhtar's wife Baha, taken to hospital in Algiers with heart trouble, and wondered if Nama was similarly afflicted.

As I watched the three of them talking, I absorbed a lesson on the complex way in which the veil acts as a symbolic manifestation of role and status. Various forms of cousin-marriage have traditionally been preferred in Tuareg society, and one of the more interesting consequences is that Tuareg are often related to one another in more than one way. Mokhtar and Kaouadis, for instance, were related by marriage, as brothers-in-law, and by blood, their fathers having been brothers, as parallel cousins. This sort of multiple relationship can place an individual in an ambivalent and even potentially contradictory social position, and the veil is one way in which it is mitigated. With regard to every other man present, each man in a group of Tuareg will stand in one or probably more than one relationship or degree of kinship – like Mokhtar and Kaouadis – to each of which a difficult level of respect is due and from each of which a different behaviour is expected. A man will unambiguously signify his awareness of his standing vis-á-vis the others at any given moment in the conversation, or when another person enters the group, by readjusting his veil – or by merely making the gesture of doing so – in relation to the adjustment of those of the people with whom he is talking. As Mokhtar, Kaouadis and Nama chatted away, I was fascinated by the almost constant subtle touches each man gave his veil. It was almost like a secret language, one impossible to understand without a profound knowledge of an extraordinarily complex kinship and social system.

From what I had already seen in Tamanrasset, it was clear that the traditional meaning and usage of the veil were becoming things of the past; indeed, many Tuareg like Bahedi (who might be regarded as an extreme example of modernity) were now spending much of their time unveiled. Even among these ultra-modernists, however, I had noticed that the veil, still worn when they were immersed in their own social and kinship network, retained something of its traditional symbolic meaning. It seemed to me that the marked decline observable in the traditional wearing and usage of the veil reflected the decline and breakdown of Tuareg social and kinship systems. With cousin-marriage on the decline in an increasingly modern and Islamised state, the ambivalence of kinship and social roles is decreasing in consequence. Furthermore, among younger Tuareg the belief systems associated with such things as the Kel Asouf, *tehot* and the shamefulness of the mouth are beginning to be regarded as belonging to an outmoded world. Yet here with Mokhtar, Kaouadis and Nama I was once again privileged to see the veil being used in its full range of symbolic and communicative meanings. It was exciting, a little cameo of the past.

I knew from Mokhtar that Kaouadis was also a Gardien du Parc, and I was keen to hear from his own lips what this involved. 'I was with the Public Works Department in Djanet [Tassili-n-Ajjer] for four years,' he said, 'then at Illizi for two years and Ghat [in Libya] for three. That was up to ten years ago.' There he stopped.

'And then you began working for the Park?' I enquired. I knew that for some Tuareg the 'Hoggar National Park', as the area had been designated in 1987, was a touchy subject.

'Oh, no,' interjected Mokhtar. 'He doesn't work for the Park.' By now I was confused. 'He doesn't *work* for the Park,' Mokhtar elab-orated, 'he is just paid by it.'

The confusion was largely of my own making, a result of my lack of fluency in Tamahak and the translation of the French word *travail* as 'work'. As far as I know, there is in Tamahak no direct equivalent of the word *travail* – which is not surprising, since in traditional Tuareg society 'work' was an alien concept, something undertaken by slaves or, in the case of agriculture, by *harratin*. I had, I now realised, failed to pick up on a clue Mokhtar had given me earlier in the day. When he was preparing lunch for us both at Adjelil Tarhaouhaout I had asked him whether he enjoyed cooking, and his response was a soliloquy on the manifold charms of the *travail* involved in being a cook and guide: that is to say, free (and guilt-free) lunches during Ramadan, and the opportunity to pay social calls on whomsoever he chose.

For both Mokhtar and Kaouadis, as for many other Tuareg, being Gardiens du Parc involved no more than continuing to live their tra-ditional semi-nomadic existence, with the slight added encumbrance of having to make the journey to Tamanrasset every once in a while to receive their payments, which I calculated averaged out at about £70 a month, depending on the number of a man's dependents and various other social circumstances. It was a designation productive of much mirth. Comments such as 'Who are you guarding the Park against?' or 'What are you guarding today?' were irrestistably amusing when the sole duty involved was to ensure that Ahaggar (the Park) was kept in its traditional state. With the almost total cessation of tourism, this now consisted of nothing more onerous than remaining alive.

It was easy to joke about it, but the Algerian government's creation of a National Park in Ahaggar, and its current policy of employing some 550 Tuareg, mostly Kel Ahaggar, as Gardiens du Parc and Chefs du Poste, has it seems to me been an ingenious and successful social and political strategy. Although a revolt by Algeria's Tuareg has always been most unlikely, it is a possibility the government has never dis-counted. Paying them to remain themselves has done much to com-pensate nomadic Tuareg for the loss of tourist income over the last decade, and thus ensure political stability in the region.

Nevertheless, from what I could gather there were a few Tuareg – Khabte had been one – who had refused to become Gardiens du Parc, considering it demeaning to take government handouts.

Looking around their camps, I found it difficult to imagine how families such as these could have survived in their semi-nomadic existence without the government's Park policy, which in the current tourist dearth had become to all intents and purposes a form of social security. Their goats provided some basis for subsistence, but with virtually nothing to trade other than their goats and no income from tourism, they had no means of acquiring the money necessary to buy wheat flour and other essential foodstuffs. Occasionally they might find work away from Ahaggar, as Fata's husband had in Ideles, but work, even in Tamanrasset, was hard to find. I couldn't help but conclude that without this active government policy there would be very few nomads left in Ahaggar, nothing but widespread and abject poverty and the danger of political unrest throughout the region.

The pragmatic side to this 'aid', if 'aid' is the right word, was encapsulated for me by Bahedi during a conversation we had had in Tamanrasset about the possible regeneration of tourism in the region. 'Without nomadism', he had said, 'there is no tourism. And without tourism there is no nomadism.' In the absence of tourism, the government's policy of propping up 'nomadism' in this way can be seen as far-sighted, a means of safeguarding the conditions for its regeneration.

That evening was New Year's Eve. I spent it with Mokhtar, Kaouadis and Nama, mostly listening to them talking. As I listened, I realised that such talk was probably the most treasured form of social intercourse in their lives, so much of which were spent either alone in the desert or at best in their own small encampments, miles from the nearest neighbours. When nomads gathered, the first word spoken after the customary words of greeting was nearly always '*Isalan?* – What news?' But it was more than a simple enquiry after news: it was an invitation to talk. And Mokhtar, Nama and Kaouadis had been talking, largely without saying anything of any great consequence, since our return from Adjelil Tarhaouhaout. I was not surprised that Nama was treated by the two men as an equal, for that was only fitting in a society with such a strongly matrilineal tradition. It was now after eight in the evening. We had eaten and drunk tea and were sitting around the fire Kaouadis had built in a natural grotto between the massive roots of three tamarisk trees behind the *oued* bank. It was snug – I was suddenly reminded of Ratty's place, in *The Wind in the Willows* – and kept out the worst of the cold. I had even managed to set up my tent within it.

On one side of the fire Nama lay, leaning on her elbow, between her brother and husband. I sat on the other. After a while Mokhtar undid the knot in the tail of his *chech*, pulled out the small plastic pot of ash he had told me was a medicine, and handed it to Nama. She sat up and delicately shook the fine black ash onto the back of one hand so that it formed a circle around an open abscess I had noticed earlier. With the forefinger of her other hand she then slowly and carefully brushed the ring of ash closer and closer to the abscess until it finally enveloped it. I wondered what properties the ash contained.

The three of them soon became absorbed in what I assumed was some sort of game involving matchsticks, the nature of which I was quite unable to grasp. There were two boxes of matches: with Mokhtar looking on like some sort of referee, Nama took one box, Kaouadis the other, and each carefully counted the matches in his or her respective box – two – four – six – eight – ten – and so on. When the counting was finished each pile of matches was put back in its box, and the boxes were exchanged, Kaouadis handing his to Mokhtar and Nama passing hers to Kaouadis, leaving her as the referee. I watched for a quarter of an hour at least, during which time half a dozen counts took place, then asked Mokhtar how the game was played.

'There are only forty-two matches in each box,' said Kaouadis, peevishly. 'There should be fifty.'

'I don't follow,' I said, not sure I had understood him.

'They're robbing us. There were always fifty in a box.'

I suddenly realised it had not been a game, but serious business.

'Pass me a box,' I said to Mokhtar, and scrutinised it carefully. Small print on one side said: 'average contents 40'. 'It's all right,' I said to Kaouadis. 'There should only be forty matches in the box, so you're better off by two.'

'That's just it,' said Kaouadis. 'There were always fifty before. It's a rip-off.' He could not be shaken from his conviction that the government had debased the value of matches – like everything else. Mokhtar and Nama agreed with him. They were probably right.

After that Nama got up, said goodnight to Mokhtar and me, and went up to her tent. (When we first arrived at this camp, I saw that Nama and Kaouadis had a military-looking tent just like Fata's. The government mark was clearly visible, stamped on its side in large print. More 'aid'?) It was getting very cold, and in spite of the fire I felt like following suit. I was about to make my move when Kaouadis fanned the embers and put on the kettle to make more tea. I stayed, and there ensued what proved to be a most extraordinary conversation. Alas! I misunderstood many of their opening remarks, so I do not know what set it off, but as I listened it seemed to develop into a compilation – 'an argument over' would be more appropriate – or inventory of almost every tribal name that had ever existed in Ahaggar, punctuated with references to camels, wells, mountains, and other place names. I listened intently, trying to figure out what they were saying about tribes; from what I remembered, some of those they mentioned had petered out generations ago. They were evidently set for the night, and after a while, curiosity overcoming my desire to get out of the cold and into my sleeping bag, I asked them what it was all about.

'Yes, you can perhaps help us,' said Mokhtar. 'You know the history of the Tuareg.' (Introducing me to Mokhtar, Bahedi had explained about my book.)

'I'm not sure,' I said. 'I don't even know what you are talking about.'

'The cause of the war,' he said, clearly assuming that I had been following their argument. After a moment of bafflement, happily, the penny dropped: they must be arguing about a famous war among the Tuareg themselves. By any yardstick it had been a 'great' war, over three years between 1875 and 1878 and involving the whole of Ahaggar and the adjoining federation of the Kel Ajjer who inhabit the Tassili-n-Ajjer and surrounding lands to the north-east.

The cause of the war, its course and its outcome were 'typically Tuareg', with all the ingredients of a medieval romance – the tears of beautiful women, the chivalry and valour of noble warriors, the cunning of traditional raiders, and the final dissipation of energy once the initial cause had been lost in trivialities along the way.

Mokhtar might just as well have asked me what caused the First World War. The answer was similarly complex, and began the same way: 'On the face of it, very little!' The great Tuareg war had its roots in the seventeenth century when the Imenan Tuareg who ruled this part of the Sahara as sultans – not a title held among the northern Tuareg today – from their power-base centred on Ghat in south-west Libya were overthrown by the noble Tuareg Uraren tribe. The Uraren became all-powerful in Ajjer, and by 1875 there were no more than seven direct descendants of the Imenan sultans left. After fleeing from the Uraren the Imenan had settled with their women (who were renowned among all the Tuareg for their beauty) and their few remaining followers in the oasis of Djanet, about three days' journey over the Tassili plateau from Ghat, and pastured their herds in the territory adjoining Ahaggar.

The Imenan at Djanet were left with only a few vestiges of their former power: a few small vassal descent groups, a small number of their Negro guards, some petty tribute payments, protection rights and duties over caravans passing down to Niger from Tripolitania, and rights over a well at Djanet. Whether from greed or as a matter of conscience or perhaps even from embarrassment must remain a subject for conjecture, but whatever the reason, the Uraren were still jealous of the lingering shadow of power cast by the Imenan's few remaining rights and by the carefully-nurtured arrogance rooted in their consciousness of their noble origins, and were intent on provoking a quarrel that would lead to the final humiliation and destruction of the Imenan. As a first step, the throats of the cattle grazed by the Imenan in a valley near Ghat were slit. The intervention of religious men from both tribes succeeded in averting a flare-up into full-scale fighting. The Uraren's next moves were to seize part of the Imenan's remaining tributary payments, to raid the Tripolitanian caravans whose safety the Imenan guaranteed, and to lay claim to the well at Djanet. This last seems to have been the final straw. In desperation the Imenan packed up and rode to the camp of the Amenukal (supreme chief) of the Kel Ahaggar, El Hadj Akhmed, to implore his help.

The small band of Imenan, accompanied by their women, must have been a piteous and moving sight as they invoked their long-lost ancestral heritage and pleaded their case before the Kel Ahaggar. And indeed, the tears and lamentations of those beautiful women filled the Kel Ahaggar with compassion and inspired in them a zeal to avenge their cause. In the face of a unanimous outcry from his people, El Hadj Akhmed had no alternative but to write to the chief of the Kel Ajjer, setting out the cause of the Imenan and asking that justice be done. But the Uraren refused to yield in the matter of the well or the Tripolitanian caravans.

For the first time in their history, all the tribes of Ahaggar rose up together. Warriors from all the noble tribes, attended by their best vassals and armed with the traditional *takouba* (broad-sword), daggers and lances (several, it seems, also carried muskets), rode on the oasis of Ghat, a combined force of 650 men. Since the total population of Ahaggar in 1860 was estimated at around three thousand, there can have been few able-bodied men who did not take up arms. Nine hundred were assembled at Ghat to meet them. The Kel Ajjer and the men of Ghat suffered a resounding defeat, but this was only the first round. The Kel Ahaggar in their turn soon suffered a crushing defeat at the hands if the Kel Ajjer, only to raise an even bigger army, eight hundred men drawn from every tribe in Ahaggar, and inflict a further defeat on the Kel Ajjer. Both sides grew enfeebled, their fighting spirit ebbed, and the war dragged its weary way to an end. The Kel Ahaggar were able to claim what was effectively no more than a Pyrrhic victory for the now sole surviving descendant of the Imenan sultanate.

One consequence of the war was that it so weakened the Kel Ahagger that the French were more easily able to conquer them less than fifteen years later.

A second consequence was that it allowed the Turks, who with this end in view had supported the Kel Ajjer, to build a garrison in Ghat and establish themselves in the Central Sahara. This had implications for the future, as it later gave the Turks a strong vested interest in supporting the fanatical Senussi religious order who within a few months of the outbreak of the First World War were in revolt against the Italians (who had by then taken over Ghat) and the French. By 1917 the Senussi-inspired revolt against the 'infidels' was so widespread that General Laperrine was transferred from the battlefields of the Somme to take command of all French Saharan territory. One can only guess what might have happened if certain small but key factions amongst the Kel Ahaggar Tuareg had not remained loyal to France.

'Women,' I said. 'They were the cause of the war. The same old story: Tuareg chasing after beautiful women!' Neither Mokhtar nor Kaouadis apparently followed my attempted banter, so I reminded them of the role of the Imenan women.

'Ah, yes,' said Mokhtar. 'That's right – but I thought it was the Taitok!' I could see exactly where the pair of them were wanting to take the discussion, but I was not willing to get involved, for I was pretty sure it would carry on throughout the night – and it was freezing. The Taitok had spent much of the nineteenth and into the twentieth century, until quite a few years after the French arrival, vying for supremacy with the Kel Rela, the other main noble descent group in Ahaggar. For their almost continuous rejection of French authority, they were eventually banished to Niger. However, since arriving back in the region I had sensed something of a revivalist movement in favour of the Taitok. Characters tough enough to resist the French for so long (unlike the Kel Rela) and to suffer banishment rather than submit were bound to be popular figures in an independent Algeria. Mokhtar and Kaouadis – and, as I was to discover, many other Tuareg – might be only too keen to do a little recasting of history regarding the Taitok, but I could no longer take the cold. I crept into my tent.

It was an hour or so before midnight, and I lay in my sleeping bag, slowly growing warm and thinking about the Millennium celebrations which were passing me by. For a moment I felt decidedly lonely, wondering what I was doing in the middle of the Sahara without my family at such a time. But then, as I thought back on the evening, I began to realise how rare and special were such company and such conversations. They held a greater depth and wealth of values than the shallow modern world, and the few remaining corners in which they could be found were fast disappearing.

I sent myself to sleep by trying to rank in fitting order the most infamous and most admirable people of the twentieth century. I couldn't decide as between Stalin and Hitler, nor was I sure where to place Margaret Thatcher on the list, and I didn't get very far with the virtuous because there were so many of them. Eventually I plumped for Poland's Marshal Piłsudski to head my 'merit' list: without his intervention, Lenin's Red Army might well have overrun Western Europe, and not only had a great racehorse been named after him, but about half the Poles I have spoken to have never heard of him. European history is a bit like that.

6

Mertoutek
the 'Garamantes' song

THE FIRST DAY of the new millennium was of no interest to either Mokhtar or Kaouadis, and to my surprise I felt similarly unmoved. Perhaps I was slightly hung-over from our late night. I had eventually fallen asleep around midnight, but suspected that Mokhtar and Kaouadis had carried on talking into the early hours. When we eventually got up, a good hour after sunrise, everyone in the camp – including the children – seemed rather lethargic. On the whole, I'm inclined to think it had more to do with the weather than anything else. Not a drop of rain had fallen in Tefedest, so Mokhtar assured me, for about four months: was the fact that it did so this of all mornings perhaps an omen for my journey? It was not heavy rain, nor the steady, gentle rain that is good for pasture, but rain in intermittent drops that seemed to have been wrung (rather than simply falling) from the cold, dank mist that completely enveloped the Tefedest. At ground level it was merely gloomy, but above us the visibility was reduced to perhaps a hundred metres and we peered into low mist and cloud. It was bitterly cold, and I was pretty sure we would see snow on the peaks if the cloud lifted. Snow is not unheard-of on the very high mountains of Ahaggar: on this very day, fifty years ago, Louis Carl and Joseph Petit's expedition was forced to take shelter from a snow blizzard in rocks only a few kilometres from where we were now. A strange coincidence.

The climate in the Sahara has not always been what it is now. Roughly ten to twelve thousand years ago the last Ice Age came to an end and the Sahara, which had been perhaps even drier and certainly colder than it is now, began to become both warmer and wetter. Rainfall in the high mountains of Atakor may have reached as much as 50 centimetres a year, in the Tassili around half as much, and here in the Tefedest probably something between the two. In the high mountains and the Tassili the vegetation was a mixture of Mediterranean and temperate species of olive, oak, hop, elm, reed, alder and chestnut. And, of course, there were the cypresses. The few still to be found growing today in the Tassili are a legacy of this era. As the climate of Ahaggar improved, so the human population increased and spread out, living mostly on the plains, along river valleys and in the low foothills below the Tassili. They also made use of the caves and natural rock shelters afforded by the weathered granites and sandstones of these mountains and plateaux, probably as they moved their herds between plain and mountain according to pasture and perhaps season.

It was one such shelter Mokhtar had promised to show me this morning. It was not far away, nor difficult to reach, but the walking and climbing involved were a bit laborious, so that it took us two or three hours to get there. The cave was one of several at the head of the valley we had just ascended, most of them formed by huge granite boulders tumbling quite higgledy-piggledy on top of each other, leaving natural shelters and caves beneath. Not all had paintings inside. Mokhtar kept well ahead of me, darting to left and right as he searched among the boulders for the right cave, repeatedly assuring me that the paintings really were here. He finally found the cave – quite well hidden, about fifteen metres above the valley floor and above a wide, sloping ledge. Its entrance was quite small, so that we both had to stoop to enter it.

'Here,' he said. 'These are good paintings, don't you think?'

'Fantastic,' I agreed, glancing around the cave. Mokhtar knew I wanted to see prehistoric rock art, and had hoped to please me by bringing me here. I did not want to disillusion him but, compared to most of those in the Tassili-n-Ajjer, where I was planning to go in a week or so, these examples were neither exceptional nor even particularly interesting. Painted in red, they were mostly of cattle and hunting scenes, and probably belonged to what is generally known as the Bovidian period, which lasted from roughly seven thousand years ago, when the domestication of animals appears to have become widespread in this part of the Sahara, to about three thousand years ago, when aridity once again set in.

I was touched by Mokhtar's concern that I should be pleased with the paintings, but also saddened by the fact that, like most Kel Ahaggar I have known, he was not particularly interested in these prehistoric paintings, not even as a Gardien du Parc.

There are, I think, a number of reasons for this lack of interest. Certainly today's Tuareg have no particular artistic leanings or traditions. Most work which involved any artistry, such as the ornamentation of leather goods, the making of jewellery and the engraving of swords and other metals, used to be done for the Tuareg by a blacksmith caste (*eneden*) who no longer form a part of the nomadic milieu, most having gravitated to the tourist markets elsewhere in the Sahara. Some are involved in modern, small-scale metalworking businesses such as auto-repairs.

Another more pertinent reason is that most Tuareg are aware that these rock paintings and engravings are the work of a people who lived in the region long before they did, and with whom they have little or no connection. Significantly, the Kel Ahaggar's own legends and myths focus more on the origin of and justification for the noble–vassal relationship than on where they originated and from whom they may be descended. Essentially these myths relate to an immigrant rather than an indigenous population, and in this bear some relation to reality. The ancestors of the present-day Tuareg were probably descended from the ancient Hawarra Berbers of Tripolitania, Cyrenaica and the Fezzan, for around AD 1050 the Hawarra of the Fezzan moved into the Central Saharan massifs of Tassili, Ahaggar and Aïr to escape the Arabic Hilal invasion of the Fezzan. This fragmentary picture, derived from Arab authors of the Middle Ages, suggests that there was an indigenous population in these massifs. Ask any Tuareg today and he will probably tell you that before his people's arrival Ahaggar was inhabited by the Isebeten, pagans who lived in mountain caves and subsisted mainly by hunting and goat-breeding. The Dag Rali, indeed, traditional inhabitants of Atakor, the high central mountains of Ahaggar, believe that they are the direct descendants of the Isebeten; ironically, perhaps, there is very little prehistoric rock art in Atakor, and the Dag Rali, lamentably but unsurprisingly, show no more interest in the subject of prehistoric rock art than do other Kel Ahaggar.

My own view is that the understandable failure of an immigrant people to embrace as their own the artistic heritage of those they supplanted was exacerbated by the French constantly telling the Tuareg that this magnificent prehistoric cultural legacy, whose virtues they extolled, had nothing to do with them. An illiterate, nomadic camel herdsman would probably see no reason to disagree with an eminent professor of archaeology. It is interesting that in Libya, so archaeologists have told me, many Tuareg express a contrastingly real sense of cultural ownership of the prehistoric rock art of their region.

I sat with Mokhtar in the cave, and as we looked at the paintings on its walls we ran our fingers over the sixteen or more (some had been eroded) intricately crafted little potholes just inside the cave entrance, about the size of inkwells, and set roughly in the shape of a draughts board. The cave's former occupants – Neolithic man – had clearly made them for a purpose, but one we could only guess at. 'Perhaps it is where they made their paints,' suggested Mokhtar, as intelligent a guess as any.

'They must have been very small people,' he said in all seriousness, as he tried to stand upright in the cave.

'They probably were,' I said. 'Although even if they weren't, I don't think they could do much about the height of the cave. Even so, it wasn't a bad place to live, eh?'

'They could sit up here all day long, just watching their animals grazing in the valley.'

'Only if they had binoculars.' Mokhtar laughed, aware that I was teasing him.

We sat in the cave entrance for about an hour, gazing down the valley just like Neolithic man. Even now it looked quite idyllic, with its sweep of acacia trees and mountainous backdrop; we speculated about what it might have been like to live here in those days, with good pasture, trees and running water. It may perhaps have been the first time that Mokhtar had ever had such a conversation, but it clearly interested him. Yes, I thought: if the French had spent more time sharing the knowledge gained from their archaeological research into the prehistory of the region with the Tuareg, these people might not now feel so detached from it.

The cloud had lifted; tiny specks of snow could indeed be seen on the highest peaks, and the warmth of the sun was beginning to make itself felt. I was sitting in one of the most remote and beautiful places on earth, in the abode of Stone Age man, having a private peep into the antechamber of one of the world's great art galleries, in the company of a man who embodied the last vestiges of nomadic culture.

Mokhtar was in particularly good form as we left the cave and walked back down the valley, chatting about anything and everything. I like to think that his chirpiness was stimulated by our discussion of rock art, and perhaps it was; but more likely he felt that, having taken me to see 'unknown' rock paintings, he was now justified in spending some time on his own social itinerary. So it was that over the next few days we visited a number of other camps along the eastern side of the Tefedest. This was not at all disagreeable for me. I was enjoying Mokhtar's company, and just now much more interested in today's Tuareg than in the rock art of the Tefedest.

The people we visited were mostly Ait Lowayen, kinsmen of Mokhtar's who were camped along the edge of the Tefedest. Most of them were not far from Adjelil, and we stayed on there, Sid Ahmed driving us out each day to the other camps. One was that of Mokhtar's mother-in-law, an old lady named Gaga. All the men of the camp – her son Adjadj, her son-in-law Fendu and her twenty-year-old grandson Mohamma – were away in the Ideles region, looking for camels. One morning Mokhtar and I joined Gaga's daughter-in-law Suna and unmarried granddaughter Marta in taking the goat herd to the nearby *guelta* for watering, and then on to graze along the lower slopes of the Tefedest. At first the two women were shy in my presence, but when they learnt that I had once spent much time in Kel Ahaggar camps, they relaxed and became very talkative. It seemed that goat herding was not so very different now from when I was last here. Three main changes had immediately struck me in visiting the camps: the tents were now mostly that standard government issue – and very commodious; the staple of their diet, which thirty years ago was *esink* (millet), was now *tagella* (wheat flour), a result of the end of the caravan trade to

Niger and the comparatively lower price of flour in Algeria; and, as in much of the rest of Africa, powdered milk rather than breast milk seemed to be preferred for babies. There was also a good supply of goat's milk in the camps, a rarity during the late 1960s and early 1970s because of the widespread drought.

Mokhtar, of course, was in his element, doing the social rounds and distributing largesse (in the form of our food supplies, for which Bahedi and I had made provision), and fulfilling his role as a Gardien du Parc – he was actually escorting a tourist around the region. His kudos was much enhanced and his social standing certainly rose a few notches, while I could not have had a better *entrée* into these camps. Accompanied as I was by Mokhtar, I was able to find out almost everything I wanted to know about the state of nomadism in the region: the problems with camels, the changes to land rights since I was last here, the impact of the loss of tourism, the lack of employment opportunities, and so forth. And whenever Mokhtar got carried away, Sid Ahmed had usually been listening and was able to give me a better perspective. Just after we had left Gaga's camp, for example, as Mokhtar came to the end of a long explanation of the tribal relationships in the area between the Ait Lowayen, Isekkemaren and Kel Rezzi Tuareg, Sid Ahmed commented that all the nomads were now *mélangé*. What he meant was that tribal differences were no longer so pronounced or so important, especially since the government had put an end to all forms of exclusive tribal land rights.

At last, with our food supplies dwindling and the rendezvous with Bahedi beckoning, we thought it time to make our way back to the village of Mertoutek. But we planned to go the slow way, stopping at the little settlement of Dehine for one night on the way. I had never been to Dehine before; all I knew was that Mokhtar lived there for some of the year, and had more kinsmen there. Getting the Land Rover into Dehine was not easy. For the first part of the journey we retraced our route southwards from Adjelil down the plain along the eastern base of the Tefedest. After thirty kilometres or so we turned in towards the mountains, following a wide, sandy, tamarisk-strewn *oued* which suddenly narrowed into a rocky defile full of oleanders, dense reeds, sedges and running water: we had reached a geological barrier similar to the one at Adjelil Tarhaouhaout. The main difference was that the *oued* here at Dehine was narrower, and the water ran on the surface for half a kilometre. Sid Ahmed eased his way forward. As far as possible he followed the natural water-course, but at times he found his way impeded by thick vegetation, and had to climb the steep rock banks to get past it.

Suddenly, just when it seemed that we could go no further, Mokhtar, who was riding in the back, banged on the cab roof for us to stop. Climbing down, I followed Mokhtar and Sid Ahmed through the reeds and up the slope of a small rocky promontory, to find myself in a most exquisite little garden bounded on one side by a thick wooden fence of broken tamarisk and thorn tree branches and on the other by the rock wall of the valley side and a water-channel that fed the little garden beds. Mokhtar, suddenly all action, pulled away great swathes of dead branches to reveal an enormous cache of melons. They were the same kind as those we had collected from Adjelil Tarhaouhaout, but whereas those were motley and few in number, these were splendid specimens, almost the size of a water-melon, but waisted and bulbous, more like a butternut squash, and with quite remarkably tough green skins – even hurling one to the ground would not break it. When eventually I was able to sample one of these prodigies, it seemed indeed more squash-like than melon-like – they have no particular fragrance, while the flesh is rather hard, and almost bitter to the taste when raw; boiled, it adds a delicate but somewhat anonymous 'vegetable' flavour to a meal, not at all unlike boiled marrow. We formed a chain, Mokhtar throwing them over the wood barricade to me and I to Sid Ahmed, who stashed them into the back of the Land Rover. Altogether we picked about two dozen. They filled the back of the Land Rover, and must have weighed at least a hundred kilos altogether.

'Whose are these?' I asked Sid Ahmed, assuming that someone from Mertoutek had commissioned him to collect them while he was passing through Dehine.

'It's my garden,' said Mokhtar, with a note of surprise in his voice, as if he had expected me to know that he had such a place. I was quite taken aback. All the time I had been with Mokhtar he had made no mention of his garden, and I had thought he was almost entirely nomadic, breeding goats and camels and picking up his 'social security' as a Gardien du Parc.

'I didn't know you worked the land,' I said rather clumsily, hoping he would enlighten me as to how he, a Tuareg, came to be engaged in what was traditionally the work of slaves or *harratin*.

'Oh yes, I have had a garden here for a long time. I live here and work it for several weeks in the year. It's good to have a garden.' This was progressive talk – at least, it certainly would have been thirty years ago. I was in Ahaggar when the first few Tuareg realised that, their traditional land rights and slaves having been taken from them, they would have to work the land themselves if they wanted garden produce. It was regarded as the most menial of all work. In the first great battle of the Kel Ahaggar–Kel Ajjer war, the Kel Ajjer, advancing provocatively towards the Kel Ahaggar, had hurled clods of earth at the Amenukal – the ultimate insult!

As we made our way at snail's pace towards Dehine, Mokhtar explained the transformation, during the last thirty years, which saw many Tuareg now happily working the land alongside former slave and *harratin* gardeners. But I gathered that acceptance of the situation was by no means universal, and that one could usually tell from the quality of the work which gardens were worked by Tuareg and which by former 'professionals'. 'I will show you tomorrow in Mertoutek,' Mokhtar said. 'You will see what I mean.'

Just when I was beginning to wonder how we were going to extricate ourselves from the *oued*, it opened out into a small basin with about a dozen *zeribas* or reed huts on either side. Those to the south belonged to Ait Lowayen Tuareg, most of whom were Mokhtar's kinsmen, while those to the north of the *oued* belonged to their former slaves. Although, as I discovered, there was extensive socialising between the two sides of the valley, the physical positioning of the dwellings and the language used (the Tuareg still referred to their neighbours as *iklan*, slaves), the distinction between the Tuareg and their former slaves was clearly still very relevant, at least socially.

The other striking feature of Dehine was Mokhtar's eldest son. Mohammed had just returned from three months' work in an office in Illizi and was sporting the latest fashion: a bright red *chech* and veil, ski glasses which hid the remainder of his face, and a brand-new black leather jacket. Had I bumped into him in a back alley in London, I should have run the proverbial mile; here, I thought he did much to enliven and jollify his setting. He was both charming and well-spoken, and it was interesting to hear his opinion of the 'outside world', and his hopes and plans to buy a four-wheel drive. That night we ate around the hearth outside the *zeriba* of Mokhtar's brother and in the company of a number of his other kinsmen. A strong wind having picked up in the course of the evening, I pitched my tent with some difficulty in the lee of an old *zeriba* no longer in use. By morning the wind had dropped, and we left early for Mertoutek. I was sorry to see that Mohammed had reverted to traditional garb.

Sid Ahmed took us on a short-cut to Mertoutek through some back valleys and cols, past a huge boulder standing on its own, the size of a large house, which had split in two, leaving a defile perhaps a metre wide in the middle through which a man could clamber. How it got here was as much of a mystery to the Tuareg as to anyone else. Generations of Tuareg over the years had inscribed their names and messages in *tifinagh* onto almost every facet of the boulder – the sort of 'rock art' with which both Mokhtar and Sid Ahmed could identify. The boulder was certainly an impressive sight, and I wanted to show my appreciation of it. My student notes flipped up lazily in my mind's eye. Discarding the 'pre-Cambrian granites' as uselessly precise, I told Mokhtar it was one of the oldest rocks in the world. He liked the sound of that.

'How old is it?' he asked.

'Between six hundred million and three billion [*milliard*] years.' I couldn't remember the exact figures, but they must have been something of that order, give or take a few million. I wasn't even sure whether Mokhtar had any conception of millions, let alone billions.

'And before that?'

I suddenly had a feeling of being drawn onto a different intellectual plane, one where I was likely to come a cropper. I thought fleetingly about 'Big Bang' and other theories of creation, none of which I felt very comfortable with, and knew I had no idea how to answer. But Mokhtar put me out of my dilemma: 'The *djenoun* [spirits],' he said emphatically and somewhat triumphantly, as if realising that I was stuck. 'Before the rocks, there were just *djenoun*.' That was good enough for me.

The entrance to Mertoutek is noteworthy not simply for the two cemeteries apparently identical in their size and the clay-plastered terracotta walls that surround them which flank the *piste*, but because one cemetery is for Tuareg and the other for *izeggaren*, blacks; as Mokhtar put it, 'for us and the former *iklan* [slaves]'. It would not have been remarkable in apartheid South Africa; here in Algeria, it seemed rather anomalous, but at the same time in keeping with both the history of the village and the attitude of its current inhabitants.

The immensely complex social and political hierarchy of traditional Tuareg society has been the subject of a myriad academic papers over the years. At the top were the Tuareg, the Kel Ahaggar, themselves divided into 'nobles', such as the Kel Rela, Taitok and a few smaller groups who have since disappeared; 'vassals', who preferred to be called Kel Ulli, People of the Goats, such as Mokhtar's Ait Lowayen and Khabte's Dag Rali; and a third group, the Isekkemaren, of uncertain origin and standing. A small number of religious groups were akin to the nobility in status. Traditionally the 'nobles' were the great 'warlords', aloof, in general marrying only among themselves, and reliant for their subsistence on various types of tribute from vassal Tuareg groups. Under French rule the 'nobility', in particular the Kel Rela, strove to maintain their social and political status by aligning themselves closely with the colonial administration, a parallel 'nobility' as they saw it. Though the hierarchy of Tuareg society is now largely a thing of the past, the Kel Rela – numbering only a few hundred, and mostly to be found in Tamanrasset – have capitalised on their knowledge of administration and of the region to establish themselves in various key positions in local government, tourism agencies, and so forth.

Beneath the Tuareg were the *harratin* and the *iklan*, the slaves, both often referred to by the Tuareg as *izeggar* (black) because of their predominantly black skin colour. Technically the *harratin* were free men, having been invited into Ahaggar to work the land for the Kel Ahaggar on a contract basis. Unfortunately for them, the contract on which most worked, the infamous *khamast* system, left many poorer even than slaves. The Arabic word *khamsa* means five, and the contract consisted of five parts. The Tuareg provided four of the essential means of production – land, water, tools and seed – and the *harratin* only one – labour. For this they were entitled to one-fifth of the harvest. But at harvest time a Tuareg garden-owner would camp beside his garden, to check on his four-fifths, living meanwhile, and often for long periods, on the hospitality of his contracted *harratin*. Unsurprisingly, several French colonial reports mention specifically the appalling poverty of the *harratin*.

Slaves were the property and personal chattels of their Tuareg masters, some of whom, notably the noble Kel Rela and vassal Dag Rali, were actually outnumbered by their slaves. Slaves undertook most of the 'work' involved in the traditional nomadic way of life, and in theory could be bartered or otherwise used as an exchange commodity, in the same way as livestock. They had no means of acquiring wealth, nor any inheritance rights. But even as an economic resource and heritable wealth, their lives in general were probably preferable to those of many *harratin* cultivators, for slaves were integrated into Tuareg society on a fictive kinship basis which linked them very closely and affectionately to their owners' families, and through these families to the various descent groups, or tribes, to whom they thus belonged. Indeed, as we have seen in the case of the legendarily beautiful Dassine, many Tuareg, notably several prominent Kel Rela, married slave girls in preference to Tuareg women. In 1968 I traced eighty-five living descendants of Bouhen ag Khebbi ag Adebir, the husband Dassine divorced, and the two slave girls he married on the rebound. Most of them claimed to be Kel Rela, but most other Kel Rela to whom I spoke referred to them as 'Noirs'.

The Kel Ahaggar seem to have treated their slaves particularly well, and scarcely any cases of slaves being sold or exchanged are known. Their rights were in fact considerable, and not the least was that of changing masters. A slave wishing to change masters would cut the ear of a camel belonging to the man whose slave he wished to be. The reality behind the symbolism was that a slave-owner was responsible for his slave's actions, and was therefore obliged to give the slave in recompense for the damaged camel. Since a man's treatment of his slaves had a bearing on the esteem in which he was held, in such an instance the new owner gained considerable prestige while the cast-off owner was subject to widespread ridicule. In a society in which status and prestige were all-important, such a sanction provided the slave with a powerful means of redress in the event of any ill-treatment.

In truth, many Tuareg were relieved when slavery was abolished by the newly independent Algerian government, since the maintenance of their slaves had become quite an economic burden. Many of these slaves, with no skills but those belonging to a way of life at odds with the modern world, were literally cast adrift, 'free' to be unemployed.

Censuses undertaken by the French between 1941 and 1959 put

the slave population at around 1,600, with the Kel Ahaggar at between 4,500 and 5,000. Bahedi and Claudia both thought that while the Tuareg population had perhaps more than doubled since I was last here, they were now probably far outnumbered by the descendants of their former slaves. Nor was the change just demographic: I was warned to expect a considerable inversion of the traditional social hierarchy.

Here in Mertoutek I was to find a microcosm of the sort of social change and 'inversion' that had been taking place all over the region. When I left Ahaggar in 1971, the population of Mertoutek had probably been about two hundred, perhaps less, mostly *harratin*, former slaves, and a few Tuareg. Now, as I walked around the village with Mokhtar, we estimated that the population had risen to around six hundred, the increase coming from surrounding Tuareg (Ait Lowayen, Isekkemaran and Kel Rezzi) and former slaves settling in the village. By contrast, many of the *harratin* had left to make the most of the opportunities presented by education and the growth of Tamanrasset and the Algerian economy. Within the village community itself there were just three jobs of recognised importance and status – the school teacher, the head of the *infirmerie* and the Chef du Poste of the National Park – and all three were currently held by descendants of former slaves. It was probably a pretty fair representation of the new social order.

As we walked back towards the village on the far side of the *oued* we came across a large garden area being tended by five men.

'They are superb gardeners,' I said to Mokhtar, as we watched the men working.

'Of course. But garden work is for the *izeggaren*,' Mokhtar replied. His tone hinted at more than just grudging admiration. 'They have always been the gardeners.'

The men, three of them hardly more than boys, were descendants of former slaves and belonged to a single extended family occupying a little settlement tucked away behind a spur of mountain a kilometre or so from Mertoutek. They were stripped to the waist and the sweat glistened on their black arms and torsos as they worked systematically, with the acquired skill of much practice. Mokhtar and I sat on the ground, chatting with them and watching as they cleaned the garden beds and rebuilt the water channels, ready for spring. They all knew Mokhtar, and their manner expressed the familiarity and friendliness of people who had lived in the same environment and community for generations. That he and they came from different sides of the old slave–master relationship was recognised as being part of history now, and of little further consequence. As at Dehine, there was no enmity between them, nothing more than an unstated acceptance of the fact that their origins (and perhaps their futures, if the cemeteries were anything to go by) were 'different'.

When they finally downed tools, at a little before midday, they invited us back to their settlement for tea. We walked together across the newly cleaned garden beds and over a small outcrop of rock and a tributary of the *Oued* Mertoutek to a small settlement, about half a dozen *zeribas* joined together in such a way as to form a single complex, its rooms linked by a number of open inner areas which could hardly be described as courtyards. A carpet had been spread for us in the blazing sun and there we sat while tea was made, slowly and clumsily, without the refinement to be found among the Tuareg.

As I cast my eyes around the assembled multitude, all that Claudia had told me in Tamanrasset about the penetration of Islam into the region and the consequent changing role of women, about the profligate breeding and the poverty, became startlingly alive. I counted more than forty people ranged along the two walls of the *zeriba* in front us – it was as if Mokhtar and I, and I especially, were prize exhibits on display. It was hard to believe that they all lived in this one complex. I counted five women, all of child-bearing age and all apparently pregnant, and thirty children probably less than ten years old. I had been pleasantly surprised by the healthiness of the children in the nomadic camps; several of these, however, though showing no obvious signs of malnutrition, were clearly ill.

Islam's hold on the region was much stronger than at the time of my last visit: so I had been told in Tamanrasset, and so I had seen for myself from the observance of Ramadan both there and in the camps. The former slave population in particular had embraced it, along with the Arabic language, as part of the new, modern order. It was not opportune to ask, but I suspected that this was a polygamous household, for both Bahedi and Claudia had confirmed that one of

the attractions of Islam for men – even among the Tuareg, traditionally monogamous except where slave 'marriages' were concerned –
was that it permitted up to four wives. I had previously been familiar
with hardship in the desert, especially during times of drought; this
was a scene of downright poverty, and had more to do with the new
order of things than the old.

It was midday and very hot by the time Mokhtar and I left the
complex to walk back along the dusty path to Mertoutek. Sid
Ahmed lived in the middle of the village with his wife and six young
children, but he had enough space in his house to make a room available for Mokhtar and me until we left for our rendezvous with
Bahedi the following evening.

I was so enjoying Mokhtar's company and the process of becoming
reacquainted with this society that I had not given much thought to
the local rock art sites – my primary concern was for the Tassili-n-
Ajjer sites near Djanet, some eight hundred kilometres to the east.
Since the rock art sites of the Tefedest are rather off the beaten track
and by no means as well documented or as famous as those of the
Tassili, it was doubtful that they would be the object of theft – at least
for the time being. Mokhtar, Sid Ahmed and the other Tuareg we
had met on our travels were all pretty certain that no major damage
had been inflicted on the Tefedest sites. No one had seen any evidence of obvious attempts to cut paintings out of the rock. Even so,
Mokhtar and I now decided to check out the sites in the immediate
environs of Mertoutek.

I wanted to know the extent to which prehistoric rock art was
being or had been damaged or actually stolen by tourists or others.
The despoliation of this great heritage of the region was not only a
crime in itself, but would spell suffering for the Tuareg from its effect
on tourism – should this recover from the conflicts in the north.
Before we set off that afternoon to look at the local sites, Mokhtar
took me to meet Abderahmane, the Chef du Poste for the Tefedest
National Park. In a roundabout sort of way, I presumed, this young
man, son of former slaves, was technically Mokhtar's boss – inasmuch
at least as he was in charge of the office, a square, single-room *zeriba*.
Abderahmane seemed thrilled to see me, though also a little over-
whelmed by the occasion. I suspected I was the first actual 'tourist' to
have come into his office since he took charge. I was keen to see
what this tiny outpost of bureaucracy contributed to Algeria's obses-

sion with paperwork. Abderahmane was clearly very proud of his office and devoted much care to it: everything was dusted, neat and tidy, just waiting for a visitor. He took the register of visitors out of a drawer in the desk and passed it to me. Opened in 1990, it was a cruel indictment of Algeria's crisis. I counted 370 visitors up to October 1993; thereafter there were none. Not a single tourist had been inside this little office for more than six years. During that time, some 100,000 people had been killed in the north of the country. I signed the book: the first in all those years.

It was small wonder that Mokhtar and the other Tuareg I had met were so fed up with Algeria's 'civil war' in the north. Tourism, camel-trekking through Ahaggar, was vital to their nomadic economy. When at Dehine I had asked Mokhtar if his garden was his work, his answer was what I had expected: 'Camels are Tuareg work,' he had said. 'For transport, for going to Tamanrasset and for baggage – and for tourist treks.'

'But there are no tourists,' I had said.

'No. But perhaps it will get better, and then they will return.' There was a pathetic optimism in the way he spoke about Algeria's crisis and the future.

Later in the day, as we drove up the *Oued* Mertoutek in the Land Rover with Sid Ahmed, we came across a garden similar in size to the one we had seen in the morning, but completely abandoned. I could tell that it had good soil and had once had an efficient water supply.

'What's the history of this?' I asked Mokhtar.

'It was a Tuareg – Ait Lowayen – garden,' he said, as if that explained everything.

'But why was it abandoned?'

'The pump broke, so they left,' he said summarily. 'About six years ago.' A large stone tomb and the stones of an abandoned camp site on the slope above the garden were the only other remains of their presence.

A little further up the *oued* we found a shelter in which there was a faded painting of a horse-drawn chariot. Such paintings are not uncommon – there are well over three hundred recorded sites of chariot paintings scattered across the Sahara – but their origins are the subject of much debate. At various times they have been attributed to the Romans, the Egyptians, the Greeks, the ancient Berber civilisations of North Africa, and the Garamantes, the people of the Fezzan conquered by the Romans in 19 BC. Mokhtar watched intently as I moved around the shelter trying to photograph it. 'What is that?' he asked. Apparently he had never seen a painting quite like it before.

I couldn't seem to make much progress in trying to explain either chariots, or the controversy over their presence in the Sahara. The sticking point seemed to be the horse. There are Tuareg words for horse – they are not uncommon among the southern Tuareg – but I had forgotten them and Mokhtar, insistent that he had never seen one, was not being helpful. I thought perhaps he was pulling my leg, but when I mentioned it later to Bahedi, he thought Mokhtar's ignorance conceivable – if unlikely. The fun came with the Garamantes. My suggestion that they might have been connected in some way to the ancestors of the Tuareg seemed to strike a chord, and Mokhtar spent that evening telling everyone in Mertoutek who cared to listen about the Garamantes. But I suspect it was the sound of the word 'Garamantes' rather than their history which appealed to him, for by the next day he had made up a song of sorts in which the only intelligible word was 'Garamantes' repeated over and over again.

That next day was to be our last together. We had arranged to rendezvous with Bahedi that night at Mokhtar's wife's camp down the *Oued* Mertoutek, where we had first gone to look for him. Mokhtar and I decided to spend the last day trekking through the mountains immediately to the north of Mertoutek, where he knew of caves and rock shelters in which there were both rock paintings and engravings.

Sid Ahmed dropped us off in the *Oued* Mertoutek a few kilometres above the village at about ten in the morning, and was to pick us up at an agreed point that afternoon. We climbed for almost two hours, carrying nothing but water bottles and my cameras, sometimes following narrow, almost gorge-like valleys; at others, and to my slight consternation, taking a precipitous route around the bluffs and shoulders of mountains. Mokhtar kept in front, and we didn't talk much as we climbed. His wiry body and fleet-footedness put me in mind of the Tuareg's much admired *mouflon*, the wild mountain goat that lives among the highest peaks and rockiest crags of these Saharan mountains.

The route Mokhtar was following was taking us more into the heart of the mountains than to their summits, so that when we eventually reached the area he had in mind we were on a rugged, boulder-strewn, uneven plateau at just over two thousand metres, with the summits of the main peaks still three hundred metres above us. We rested for a while, then he took me in search of the paintings. There were about a dozen caves and shelters that had probably been occupied by Neolithic man, and several of them contained paintings. But they were of a similar calibre to what I had seen the previous day, not to be compared to those I hoped to see in the Tassili-n-Ajjer in a few days' time. There was a fair amount of damage from tourists, mostly in the form of names and dates scratched on the rock and from 'washing' the paintings to enhance their colour – a process which rapidly contributes to their fading and erosion. But most of the damage seemed to have been done in the 1980s or earlier, when several hundred tourists came to Mertoutek each year. In any case, I was more interested in talking to Mokhtar. I think our activities and my company over the last week or so had whetted his appetite, because he kept telling me what he could do if tourists came back to the area. 'That's my "work",' he kept saying. 'With the camels, as a guide and a cook – *pour les allemands, les français et les autres.*'

'What about the English? Wouldn't you take *les anglais*?' I asked, ribbing him.

'Oh yes, of course, and the English. But you are the only Englishman I have met.'

I was reluctant to encourage Mokhtar to discuss the revival of tourism: it would be cruel, convinced as I was that the government's talk of ending the crisis in the north and returning the country to normality had more of hope to it than reality, and was unlikely to be realised in the near future. Tourism had more or less saved the nomadic economy in the 1960s and 1970s, and in the 1980s up to 10,000 tourists a year passed through Tamanrasset: Tuareg of Mokhtar's age now looked back on those years through rose-tinted spectacles – they were 'the good old days' – and craved a return to them. But I could not see it happening in the immediate future.

Instead, I steered the conversation to the Kel Asouf, a subject guaranteed to make Tuareg laugh. We were sitting in a fairly dark grotto. Mokhtar was wearing a *chech* on his head, but his face was completely unveiled. 'Shouldn't you have your veil up in here?' I said, as matter-of-factly as possible. He touched his veil, which was under his chin, and looked at me quizzically. 'Because of the Kel Asouf!' I said, in a bantering tone.

'*Tidet, tidet* [That's the truth]!' he cried, bursting into laughter.

'Well, what about them?'

He wouldn't give me a straight answer. It was like trying to coax a child who wanted to believe in Father Christmas to admit he knew it was his parents who filled his Christmas stocking.

'You know all about the Kel Asouf?' It was not an answer to my question.

'Of course. And the Kel Had.'

'And', he added, 'the Kel Tenere!'

'And the Kel Amadal.'

My somewhat pretentious display of erudition and apparent determination to have the last word earned their just reward. Mokhtar was no fool. He saw the trap I had wandered into, and he sprang it.

'You see, you know, then!' he said. 'The old people – maybe they still believe a little in them.' That round was definitely Mokhtar's.

I never did persuade him into an unequivocal statement that he did not believe in the Kel Asouf, but what he said was enough to confirm my guess that few Tuareg would give them much credence today – just one reason why the many symbolic meanings attached to the wearing of the veil are becoming part of history.

We left the plateau area after about an hour and began a long descent towards the *Oued* Mertoutek down a small tributary *oued* which followed a course around the back of the main block of mountains. It was full of boulders, stones and a surprising amount of vegetation in the form of thorn bushes, one or two little trees whose names I had forgotten, and quite a selection of grasses and small plants.

I remember a French ethnographer who had made a study of the subject once telling me that there were at least six hundred plant species in Ahaggar, most of them with some form of pastoral, nutritional or medicinal property. It is not a figure I have ever doubted, and as Mokhtar took it upon himself to refresh my memory of the names of all the plants that we came across in the valley, I was once again reminded of the Tuareg's extraordinarily detailed knowledge of the environment in which they live.

We were about half-way down the *oued* when Mokhtar suddenly grabbed my arm and pulled me to one side. 'Be careful!' he warned. 'You must keep away from the trees.'

'Why?' I was a little surprised.

'Because of traps. They are buried in the sand of the *oued*, attached to nearby trees.' Sure enough, concealed beneath the sand in a narrow defile between two boulders and attached to the trunk of a handy thorn tree was a steel gin-trap, powerful enough to inflict serious injury. The Tuareg had been great hunters, the *mouflon* their most cherished prize, but by the 1960s the French had hunted the wildlife of the region almost to extinction. I wondered whether the gazelle and *mouflon*, in particular, had returned during the almost forty years since their departure, and whether there had been a regeneration of hunting among the Tuareg.

'What will they hope to catch here?' I asked Mokhtar.

'Rabbit, marmot, fennec and maybe even a gazelle.'

'And *mouflon*?'

'Ah, *mouflon*,' Mokhtar sighed. 'Perhaps a *mouflon*.'

'But there are no *mouflon* here, are there?'

'There are. Oh, yes. There are *mouflon* in the Tefedest, and sometimes we catch them.' I had never seen a *mouflon* in Ahaggar thirty years ago. Had they made a come-back, or was this just another Tuareg daydream about an animal which had already entered their mythology?

It was late afternoon by the time we finally reached our rendezvous point with Sid Ahmed in the *Oued* Mertoutek, which didn't give us much time to get back to the village, pick up our things and then head off down the *oued* to where Mokhtar's wife and boys were camped, to meet Bahedi. I was rather counting on Bahedi being late, so that we could spend the night at Mokhtar's camp. And indeed Bahedi and Hosseyni were held up leaving Tamanrasset, and it was almost nine o'clock before we saw their headlights probing through the thick mass of tamarisks in the *oued*.

Bahedi's arrival made me feel quite sad, for it brought home to me that I would probably never see Mokhtar again – unless I was lucky enough to be able to make another trip. Already I had been scheming how it might be possible to get his precious binoculars to him.* As I had expected might be the case, several of Mokhtar's kinsmen were already at his camp, probably well aware that Bahedi would be returning from Tamanrasset with the substantial supplies of flour and other essentials we had agreed on with Mokhtar as payment for his services as a Gardien du Parc.

---

* He received them seven months later.

That night the talk was of the news from Tamanrasset of some sort of amnesty-cum-ultimatum the government was proposing to the 'men in the mountains' (the 'rebels'), and Mokhtar's account of our journey. When he related our discussion about In Eker, almost everyone joined in trying to compile a list of those who had died. It was interesting, and more so when the conversation turned to the question of why no action had been taken. The answer, of course, was pretty obvious: the French had clearly tried to cover it up and deny it had occurred; the Algerians, even assuming they knew about it, had just won their independence from France, and had enough problems on their plate. I don't know whose it was, but a voice from beside the fire said: 'It's because the generals, French and Algerian, have always been in cahoots with each other.' Even here, I realised, deep in a remote corner of the Sahara, people were now more aware of the ways of the world.

We left Mokhtar's camp at dawn for the five or six hours' drive back to Tamanrasset. A sad farewell was made more poignant still by Mokhtar's desire to give me something as a keepsake. I told him it was unnecessary, that he had given me more than enough, in the way of memories. But he dug around inside his tent and emerged with a cardboard teapot-holder his wife had embroidered for him. It was a very touching present.

It was good to get back to Bahedi and Claudia's *gîte*, to shower, shave and get into clean clothes. Then I set about buying an air ticket to Djanet, a small oasis town in the Tassili-n-Ajjer eight hundred kilometres east-north-east of Tamanrasset, where I planned to reacquaint myself with the best-known and most splendid of all the Sahara's prehistoric rock art.

Air Algérie has three offices on Tamanrasset's short high street, but still it took me two days to buy that ticket. Even now, I am not quite sure why it took so long. First I had to find the right office: only one of them sold tickets. When I got to the right office, it took some time to confirm that it was indeed where I should be buying my ticket. Then it was just a matter of waiting in a queue – but a queue whose tail never seemed to get much nearer to the head. Eventually, much later, I discovered that there was a ticketing system like they have in supermarket delicatessens, by which time the machine had run out of tickets. When I finally reached the counter, I thought I was in business: there was a seat on the next flight at midnight, and the ticket was written. But that was the end of the easy part. The ticket clerk told me he could not hand over the ticket until it had been paid for, and it could only be paid for at the *Caisse*. There was no queue at the *Caisse*, possibly because it was only foreigners who had to go through this rigmarole. To my amazement, however, the *Caisse* would not accept my money (Algerian dinars) without a certificate from the Central Bank confirming that I had got them from there. I protested, politely; it is a closed currency – how else could I have got any dinars, if not from an Algerian bank? That, the clerk told me, was precisely the confirmation that he needed. Catch-22 was being taken to another dimension.

I set off for the bank, only to find that during Ramadan it closed for the day at two in the afternoon. I wasn't going to make that midnight flight. When I returned the following day, it was to be told that they needed confirmation from Air Algérie of the price of the ticket. Air Algérie told me this was not necessary, but another morning was almost gone so I implored the clerk for a note and he obliged. It was good enough for the bank, and my foreign exchange document was counter-stamped to confirm that the same bank had previously exchanged my traveller's cheques. Armed with this precious document I returned once more to the *Caisse* at Air Algérie. There they were at last prepared to take my money, and it was then just a matter of getting back into the original queue and having my ticket rewritten for the next flight. And the country is desperate to attract tourists!

Yet one should not judge Algeria too harshly for such little *divertissements* as these, fruits as they are of a unique legacy of bureaucratic absurdity. Having inherited much of France's antiquated administrative system, Algeria then embellished it with bad habits picked up during post-independence flirtations with the USSR and almost every other member of the Eastern Bloc, and has subsequently failed to avoid many of the less efficient manifestations of its own various brands of socialism.

I might have lost a day in the Tassili, but I had gained one in Tamanrasset, plus two extra evenings. It was worth it. On the first evening Bahedi took me to a couple of houses in which Tuareg stayed (in the same way as they might enter a tent) when they were visiting Tamanrasset. At each house we were ushered into the main room and seated on brightly-coloured carpets spread on an immaculately clean gravel floor. These carpets and some cushions were the sole furnishings, except for a television set on a low table in the centre of one wall. Around the other three walls sat a dozen or so Tuareg. Customary greetings were exchanged as Bahedi and I took our places on the carpets, but all eyes were focused intently on the television. At this time of day the broadcasts consisted of little more than turgid political sermons in which the President or various ministers explained the government's latest attempts to end the 'civil war' in the north. For me, it was a real eye-opener. Far from being bored or uninterested, these Tuareg seemed to be both well-informed about the 'war' and supportive of *Le grand caïd Bouteflika*, as they referred to the country's President, in the struggle against the Islamic fundamentalists they blamed for the cessation of tourism.

We didn't stay more than about three-quarters of an hour in either house – just long enough, Bahedi thought, for me to appreciate the power of television! Certainly I had never imagined a day when I would see a group of Tuareg sitting in the middle of the Sahara, 'glued to the box'.

On the second evening I had the enormous pleasure of meeting Bahedi's father Mohammed for the first time. He was an old man in his late eighties but, as Bahedi warned me, still had the sharpest of minds and a wicked sense of humour.

The old man had spent most of his life in the French army as a *goumier*, or Arab auxiliary, and a fast camel rider or *méhariste*. There was not much he did not know about the Sahara, and his stories and anecdotes were well on the way to becoming part of Tamanrasset's folklore. Bahedi had already regaled me with a selection. 'You should try to record them,' I had told him. 'Some of them are gems.'

'Impossible. As soon as he realises he's being pumped, he just clams up. You've just got to wait for one of his good days and hope that he comes out with them – they really are one-offs.'

The story of Mohammed's I liked most, perhaps because it appealed to my anthropological background, was of how he had handled the Algerian government's policy on names. Tuareg were told that they could no longer continue to use their traditional system of naming, which consisted simply of a single first name added on to the father's name: Mohammed *ag* (son of) Bahedi *ag* Ahmed *ag* ... and so on – in the case of women, Fatma *ult* (daughter of)

Mohammed. Instead, they were to drop the *ag* and take a 'proper' family name.

The key feature of the traditional system was that it enabled Tuareg to trace their descent easily and relatively unambiguously over several generations, sometimes as many as seven, which was of crucial importance at a time when political power and many other rights were located strictly within lineages: membership of a particular family could be almost a matter of life or death. With the abolition of the *ag/ult* system, genealogical amnesia set in rapidly, accelerating the decline in the relevance of 'descent' as the principle upon which the social organisation of Tuareg society was based. For me, this loss of 'naming' was sadder than almost any other change I had seen among the Tuareg. Effectively their fundamental identity – their names – had been removed at a stroke. Fortunately, perhaps, I don't think many Tuareg saw it in such terms. Indeed, from what I could gather, most seem to have gone along with the change in a spirit of great good humour. Some even seized upon it as an opportunity to re-arrange their kinship ties, taking on new or getting rid of old iden-tities. One such was Bahedi's father, who really should have taken the name of Henne, like the rest of his kinsmen; but because he had a number of half-brothers and sisters to whom he was 'not very close' (as Bahedi discreetly put it) who had all taken the name of Henne, after their father and his, he had decided not to. Sharp as a new pin, Mohammed saw in the government decree a chance to distance himself once and for all from these bothersome kinsmen. He there-fore chose the name of another ancestor, Bahedi, as his family name.

There are many other such stories involving renaming. About the time of its introduction, for example, Beh ag Ahmed (now Beh Cherifi) needed a passport to visit France. When he applied for it the official who dealt with him, an Arab from the north, asked what sort of name 'Beh' was (it is pronounced 'Ba', with only a suggestion of the 'h'). 'You should choose a sensible name like Abdelazziz,' was his opinion. Beh, reluctant to fall out with the administration, thus trav-elled to France as Monsieur Abdelazziz. It took some time for him to reacquire his own name.

I met Mohammed at Bahedi's house in one of the old quarters, near the centre of Tamanrasset (it had been totally and attractively modernised, with plumbing, electricity, and modern fittings and fur-nishings). It was not a party, more a small gathering of people who had 'dropped in', several of whom I did not know. One of these, to my slightly shocked surprise, was teasing the old man about his illiteracy. When, shortly afterwards, Mohammed picked up a book and began to leaf through it, the young man was quick to point out to him that it was upside-down.

'How observant of you,' Mohammed replied blandly. 'But this way it takes me a little more time to read it, so my pleasure lasts longer.'

The young man, Ahmed, was a distant kinsman – a cousin of sorts. He affected a rather world-weary air, old beyond his years. On another occasion Mohammed, asked Ahmed's age, replied dead-pan: 'Three years older than me.'

7

Tamrit
the oldest trees on earth

A FTER THE PARTY to meet his father, Bahedi took me out to the
airport and dropped me off. It was already getting on for midnight. I passed through what seemed like even more security checks
than when I'd arrived, checked in, and went through to the embark-
ation lounge – though that is rather a courteous description.
Dilapidated seats of differing vintage and design were ranged around
the sides of the room and in two rows down the middle. It contained
nothing else save, by the exit, a wooden desk which looked as though
it might have come from a schoolroom. The flight was expected to
leave at around one in the morning.

I glanced at the man sitting next to me, a couple of seats away, as
one does. After a second, horrified look I wrenched my eyes away,
acutely aware that I was staring. My eyes had not deceived me. That
was no polo–necked sweater he was wearing – that was a band of scar
tissue. About an inch wide, it stood out from his neck by about the
same amount, running from just under his left ear to roughly where
his jugular vein was on the other side. It was grotesque, and my eyes
were drawn to it repeatedly. There was no mistaking it: the man had
been *égorgé*, and had survived. He was about thirty and looked pretty
fit in every other respect, which is possibly how he had managed to
get away, and to survive. He could easily have avoided the stares of
people like me by covering the scar with a high-collared shirt. But I
could not help thinking that he was making a statement: he wanted
everyone to see just what was going on in his country, what was

being done in the name of Islamic fundamentalism. If that was indeed his message, it went out loud and clear. The image still haunts me.

We sat there for about an hour, waiting for the flight to be called. He stared straight ahead, his face as impassive and expressionless as if he were still in shock, seemingly oblivious of the crowd of passengers around him. I would have liked to talk to him, to ask what had happened, how he had survived, and what he was doing down here in the south. His casual Western clothes – black leather jacket, white shirt and dark trousers – and particularly the absence of a head-dress seemed to suggest that he was not a local, and I wondered if he had come to Tamanrasset to escape the 'war'. Ordinarily I probably would have chatted to him – most Algerians have very interesting tales to tell – but the scar was a barrier, making me feel I had no right to intrude upon him. So I have no answers to my questions.

Once the flight was called there were three more security checks, and I noticed some helicopter gunships parked on the tarmac as we crossed it to board the plane. We eventually touched down in Djanet at 2.20 a.m. Djanet is about five hundred and thirty metres lower than Tamanrasset, and that difference in altitude made all the difference between freezing, and merely being cold: the temperature at Djanet was three degrees Celsius. I had been here before, in the mid 1960s, but in the darkness nothing looked familiar.

Hardly anyone got off the plane at Djanet; most of the passengers, including the victim of the war, continued on through the night to Algiers. Security even at this airport, little more than a landing strip in the desert, was as tight as ever. But before the police had even finished strutinising my passport and travel *fiches*, my arm was grabbed by a swarthy, powerful-looking man in his mid to late thirties. To my surprise, he was holding my rucksack in his other hand – then I realised it was not difficult to link me correctly to my baggage as it was all that had come off the plane. He told the police to stop wasting time, took my passport from them, and more or less frog-marched me out through the door and into a waiting Toyota Land Cruiser in which three leather-jacketed and equally swarthy-looking men were already sitting. Since I had been 'grabbed' under the noses of the airport police, it was unlikely that I was being kidnapped. Probably, I thought, it was the security police doing their stuff.

'You want a hotel?' It was more order than question.

1. The volcanic peaks of Atakor, looking south-east from Assekrem

2. Mokhtar (ag) Bahedi

3. Nagim

4. Mokhtar's niece with a young kid,
Adjelil camp

5. Mokhtar ag Mohammed

6. Mokhtar, Nama and Kaouadis on the night of the Millennium Eve

7. Ait Lowayen men and women sitting outside Kaouadis and Nama's tent at Adjelil. Note that the men are veiled while the women are not

8. Exploring the Tassili in the Ahellakane region. The view looks south through a passage in the upper scarp. *From left to right*: Hamed, Nagim, Moustaffa, Bahedi, Hamdi and Erza

9. Looking for a route between Erg Tihodaine (*far right*) and the Tassili scarp. Tin Haberti is the furthest mountain in the distance

10. Collecting firewood from a dead acacia on the way to Tin Ghergoh. Moustaffa and Nagim struggle to break the trunk as Bahedi gives advice. Hamed is in the background

11. Tyanaba (Jabbaren, Tassili). See page 136 for an account of the Tyanaba myth

12. 'Le Grand Dieu' at Sefar (Tassili). The effects of 'conservation' experiments undertaken by 'scientists' in or before 1968, using a synthetic resin to consolidate the rock, can be seen in two rectangular areas: on the chest of the antelope, and extending leftwards from the centre of the 'giant's' stomach to cover the hands of a suppliant woman. Dimensions: Giant's height 3.25m. Width of shelter 16m. Coverage of whole composition 30 sq. m.

13. Half of a painting chiselled out from a shelter at Jabbaren (Tassili).
Dimensions: c. 0.80–1.00 × 0.25–0.40m

14. Female figurines at Tamdjert. This picture was taken by the author in 1969. Thirty years later the painting could not be found. Whether it had been chiselled out of the rock or simply desecrated is not known

15. Tan Zoumiatak (Tassili). 'Two slender, exquisitely coiffed and bejewelled women would have enhanced the elegance of any contemporary catwalk' (see page 128). Note the 'jelly-fish/medusa' symbol to the right of the *mouflon*

16. A typical 'street' at Sefar. Beneath the sandstone pillars and walls lie rock shelters

My nervousness eased slightly. 'Yes, thank you,' I replied. 'The old Hôtel Zeriba if that is possible, not the new one.' I had heard that a new hotel had been built outside town, on the road to the airport, but I wanted to stay at the Zeriba, even though it was probably a bit decrepit and short on mod cons: it was something of an institution in this part of the Sahara.

As we drove the thirty-odd kilometres from the airport into Djanet, I discovered that the man who had effectively kidnapped me was in fact the owner of the Zeriba. His name was Abdel Khader, and his three companions were his 'brothers'. To describe it as kidnapping was going too far, of course, but I was clearly the prize in a desperate commercial struggle. Abdel Khader and his family were of Berber origin, from Ouargla, a town in the northern desert, and had bought the old Hôtel Zeriba. Shortly afterwards, it had been burnt down. Undeterred they had raised money (probably from their own family) to rebuild it, only for its completion to coincide with the onset of Algeria's crisis and the collapse of tourism. I liked what I saw of it. It had atmosphere. It was tatty and incomplete, but reminiscent of various little hotels in other Saharan oases I had stayed at many years ago. At the time, they had all conjured up pictures of the nineteenth century. There might be a growing feeling that an end to the 'civil war' was in sight, and a growing hope that tourism would pick up, but Abdel Khader faced stiff competition from the new hotel. He was at the airport to meet every flight, just on the off-chance that it might be carrying a passing traveller such as myself. I could not but admire his determination.

Though I recall being absolutely spellbound by one awe-inspiring image after another at my first encounter with the rock art of the Tassili, I now wondered if I had after all been too young to appreciate their full magnificence. The paintings in the Djanet region are generally regarded as the high point of Saharan rock art, described by the late Henri Lhote, the French ethnologist with whose name they are closely associated, as 'The world's greatest collection of Prehistoric Art'. I felt a strange sort of nervousness at the prospect of seeing these paintings again, rather like my feelings about returning to see the Tuareg, but compounded by another level of anxiety to do with the question of whether rock art was being stolen from the Tassili, as that

Internet report claimed it was from the adjoining Acacus mountains in Libya.

The theft of antiquities anywhere is a heinous and all too common crime, but perhaps even more reprehensible here in the Sahara. This great natural museum is the one asset that has been left to the Tuareg. It is the basis not just for the future prosperity of the region, but for the very survival of the Tuareg's semi-nomadic way of life. If these sites are defiled, there will be little left to attract the tourism on which the Tuareg, 'nomadism', and even townspeople like Abdel Khader are so desperately dependent.

I had given considerable thought to how such thefts might be carried out. They were unlikely to be undertaken through Algeria, I had decided. There are only four passes up on to the plateau of the Tassili-n-Ajjer from the Djanet side, and I presumed they must be pretty well guarded by the National Park, local police and tourist agencies. Even if thieves did succeed in getting onto and off the plateau on the Algerian side unnoticed, they would have little chance of travelling undetected *through* Algeria carrying baggage weighted down with rock. No – the weak link in the Tassili's security is its eastern, Libyan side. Access to the plateau from Libya is much easier: the scarp on that side of the Tassili is less pronounced and less of a barrier, and the border itself has no formal demarcation line or security checks. Libya, moreover, is desperately short of foreign exchange and currently encouraging mass tourism while doing little to prevent the accompanying damage to its antiquities. If at any time during Algeria's crisis I had been commissioned to steal Tassili rock art, I would not have approached the Tassili from the Algerian side; I would have entered and left the region by way of Libya. Though internal security generally in Algeria has been at a high level since the onset of the crisis in 1992, the Tassili itself has been left comparatively empty and unguarded. Nor has there been any risk to thieves of being disturbed by other tourists, or guides.

If rock art was being stolen from the Tassili by way of Libya, how was I to find evidence of it except by trekking from one site to another and keeping my eyes open? It was a daunting prospect: I really would be looking for the proverbial needle in a haystack. Neither was my quest something I could advertise in Djanet or even mention to my guides, for Algeria was as likely as most countries to